AF480200

THE ENTREPRENEUR'S HANDBOOK TO BUSINESS FINANCE

CORE CONCEPTS AND STRATEGY

CA N RAJA

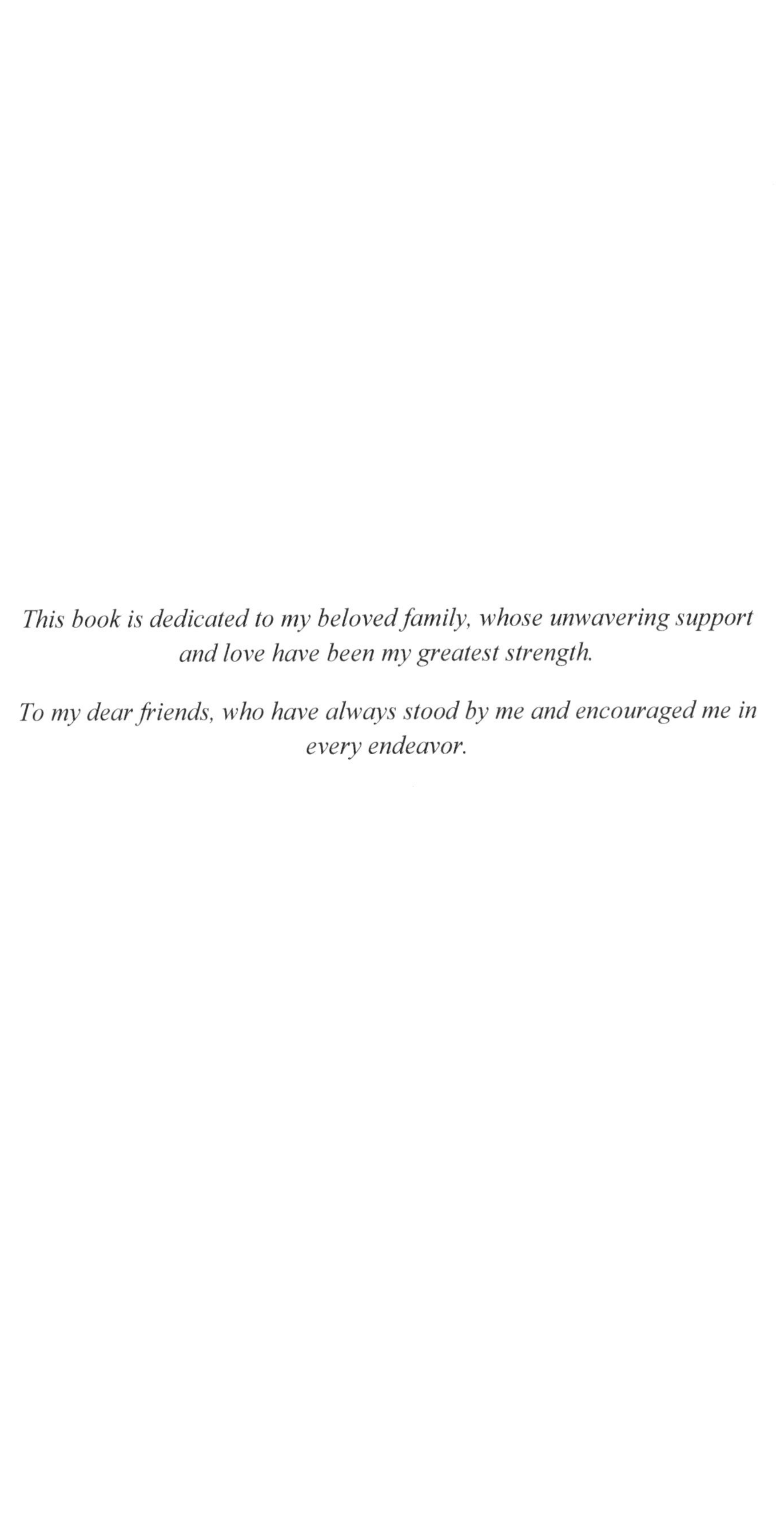

This book is dedicated to my beloved family, whose unwavering support and love have been my greatest strength.

To my dear friends, who have always stood by me and encouraged me in every endeavor.

Contents

Preface

Welcome to "**The Entrepreneur's Handbook to Business Finance: Core Concepts and Strategy.**"

Running a business is a rewarding but complex journey, and one of the most challenging aspects for entrepreneurs is managing the financial side of things. Understanding your business's financial health is crucial not just for growth but for survival. However, finance is often seen as confusing, intimidating, or something to be left to accountants.

This book is designed to break down those barriers. Instead of giving you technical jargon and dense explanations, we've structured the entire book as a conversation between two characters, **Manu** and **Vinu**. Vinu is an entrepreneur like many of you—curious, ambitious, and eager to grow his business but with lots of questions about how to manage his finances effectively. Manu, on the other hand, is the seasoned financial expert who simplifies complex financial concepts in a way that's easy to understand and apply.

Each chapter is structured as a dialogue, where **Vinu asks the questions you've probably had at some point, and Manu answers them with practical insights and real-world examples.** Together, they explore key financial areas like financial statements, liquidity management, optimising cost of capital, understanding leverage, investment decisions, etc.

By the end of this journey, you'll have the clarity and confidence to make smart financial decisions for your business. This book isn't just about theory; it's a roadmap that will guide you through every step of managing your business's finances.

Whether you're a new entrepreneur or someone who's been running a business for years, the conversations between Manu and Vinu will resonate with you. This book will serve as your companion, helping you gain a deeper understanding of the financial aspects that can take your business from surviving to thriving.

So, let's get started! Join Manu and Vinu as they explore the financial world, making it accessible, relatable, and, most importantly, manageable for every entrepreneur.

Best wishes,

CA N Raja
Banking & Finance Coach
WhatsApp: +91 9025100249
support@carajaclasses.com

Introduction

Vinu: Manu, I've been running my business for a few years now, but honestly, I always feel like I'm flying blind when it comes to the financial side of things. I focus on making sales and managing operations, but I can't say I have a solid grasp of where my business really stands financially. It feels like I'm missing something important.

Manu: That's a common feeling, Vinu. Many entrepreneurs are great at their craft, whether it's developing products or delivering services, but the financial side can be a mystery. You're not alone in feeling this way. The thing is, knowing how much money is coming in and going out isn't enough. To truly steer your business in the right direction, you need a clear view of its financial position—and that means understanding every aspect of your finances, not just the sales and expenses.

Vinu: I get that, but where do I even start? I hear terms like "cash flow," "profit margins," "leverage," and "liquidity," but I've never really understood how all of that fits together.

Manu: You've hit the nail on the head. The key is understanding how these elements work together to give you a complete picture of your business's financial health. It's like looking at a car dashboard—you can't just focus on speed. You also need to know your fuel level, engine temperature, and other indicators to make sure the car runs smoothly.

Vinu: Makes sense. But why is financial clarity so important for an entrepreneur like me? After all, I've been able to run the business so far without focusing too much on it.

Manu: True, but think of it this way: without financial clarity, you might be unknowingly making decisions that could harm your business in the long run. For instance, you might take on too much debt or miss growth opportunities because you didn't plan your cash flow correctly. On the flip side, when you **understand your financials**, you can make informed decisions—whether it's about expanding, hiring, or even weathering a tough season.

Vinu: So, financial clarity isn't just about keeping the business running day-to-day—it's about long-term decision-making?

Manu: Exactly! It's about **strategic decision-making**. Knowing your business's financial health allows you to identify where you can grow, when to take risks, and how to avoid pitfalls. You'll know when to raise capital, when to reduce costs, and how to balance growth with stability.

Vinu: Okay, I'm sold. But I still don't know where to start. What should I focus on first?

Manu: The starting point is understanding **financial statements**—your balance sheet, income statement, and cash flow statement. These documents aren't just for accountants. They're your guide to understanding how much your business is worth, how profitable it is, and whether you have enough cash to keep things moving.

Vinu: I've seen those statements, but they seem like a foreign language to me. Is it really necessary for me to understand all the details?

Manu: You don't need to become an accountant, but you should know how to interpret the key figures. Don't worry, we'll break it down step by step. Once you understand the basics of your financial position, everything else will start to make sense. You'll feel more confident in managing your business's finances and more in control of its future.

Vinu: That sounds good! So, what's next?

Manu: Next, we'll start by laying the foundation: understanding financial statements. From there, we'll move on to other key areas like **cash flow management, profitability**, and liquidity. By the end of this journey, you'll be able to make decisions that are not just based on instinct, but backed by solid financial data.

Vinu: Looking forward to it! Let's get started.

Chapter 1: Laying the Financial Foundation

1.1 The Importance of Financial Discipline for Entrepreneurs

1.2 The Importance of a Fool-Proof Accounting System

1.3 Understanding Financial Statements

1.4 Know Your Financial Metrics

A. Gross Profit Margin

B. Net Profit Margin

C. Current Ratio

D. Quick Ratio (Acid Test)

E. Return on Assets (ROA)

F. Return on Equity (ROE)

G. Debt-to-Equity Ratio

H. Debt Service Coverage Ratio (DSCR)

I. EBITDA

J. Operating Profit Margin (EBIT Margin)

K. Debtors Collection Period (DCP)

L. Inventory Holding Period (IHP)

M. Creditors Payment Period (CPP)

N. Cash Conversion Cycle (CCC)

O. Cost of Goods Sold (COGS) Ratio

1.1 The Importance of Financial Discipline for Entrepreneurs

Vinu: Manu, I'm eager to dive into Financial Statements. Shall we start?

Manu: Yes Vinu, but before we get into all the financial details, there's one key principle you need to understand—**financial discipline**. It's the foundation for managing business finances, and without it, even the best strategies can fall apart.

Vinu: Financial discipline? I always thought that was just about sticking to a budget. Is there more to it than that?

Manu: Definitely. Sticking to a budget is just one part of it. Financial discipline is about making smart, consistent choices with your business's money. It includes budgeting, yes, but also controlling spending, managing cash flow, and avoiding unnecessary debt. It's about building good financial habits that keep your business stable and growing.

Vinu: So it's about staying in control and making sure the business isn't running out of money, right?

Manu: Exactly. Think of financial discipline as the foundation of a house. If the foundation isn't solid, the house can collapse when there's a storm. Financial discipline keeps your business strong, even when challenges come up.

1. Benefits of Financial Discipline

Vinu: What are the main benefits of being financially disciplined? Is it just about avoiding financial trouble?

Manu: Avoiding trouble is one part, but financial discipline does much more than that. Here are a few key benefits:

- **Better Cash Flow**: When you monitor cash flow, you make sure the business has enough to cover daily operations and unexpected expenses. This keeps you from scrambling to pay bills or make payroll.

- **Improved Decision-Making**: Financial discipline helps you make smarter choices. For example, before expanding, you'll know if you have enough resources or if it's better to wait.

- **Increased Profitability**: You can identify areas to save money, so more of your revenue turns into profit. It's not about being cheap—it's about making sure every rupee you spend adds value.

- **Financial Resilience**: Discipline builds a buffer for tough times. With financial reserves, you can handle unexpected expenses or changes in the market without risking the entire business.

Vinu: So, being disciplined with finances makes the business more stable and prepared for the future?

Manu: That's right! Financial discipline lets you focus on growth, knowing you have a solid foundation in place.

2. Financial Discipline in Daily Operations

Vinu: How can I bring financial discipline into my daily operations? What does it look like day-to-day?

Manu: It's about staying consistent and intentional with every financial decision. Here are some daily practices:

- **Create and Stick to a Budget**: Set a budget for each area of the business—marketing, operations, etc.—and stick to it. Review the budget monthly to see if adjustments are needed.

- **Monitor Cash Flow Regularly**: Track cash inflows and outflows at least weekly. This helps you catch issues early and stay on top of finances.

- **Limit Impulse Spending**: Avoid the temptation to make spontaneous purchases. Always assess if a purchase adds long-term value to the business.

- **Set Financial Goals**: Define clear financial goals, like increasing profits by 10% or saving for expansion. Goals give you a target to work toward.

Vinu: So the key is to make these actions a habit and do them consistently, right?

Manu: Exactly. When these actions become habits, you'll automatically make better financial decisions. And along the way, stay clear of financial indiscipline!

3. Financial Indiscipline to Avoid

Vinu: What kinds of activities count as financial indiscipline? I'd like to know what to avoid.

Manu: Great question! Financial indiscipline can quickly harm a business. Here are **20 activities** to watch out for:

- **Over-relying on debt**: Using debt to cover everyday expenses can lead to high interest costs.

- **Not having an emergency fund**: Without savings for emergencies, small setbacks can become major crises.

- **Impulse buying**: Making large purchases without a plan can drain your cash flow.

- **Skipping cash flow monitoring**: If you don't track cash flow regularly, you could run into unexpected shortages.

- **Ignoring financial reports**: Not reviewing reports means missing important insights about your business's health.

- **Mixing personal and business finances**: This makes it hard to track business expenses and can cause financial confusion.

- **Not setting a budget**: Without a budget, spending can get out of control, leading to cash flow problems.

- **Making unplanned expansions**: Expanding without assessing finances can put a strain on resources.

- **Over-investing in inventory**: Having too much stock ties up cash that could be used elsewhere.

- **Not paying taxes on time**: Late tax payments can lead to fines and affect your business reputation.

- **Excessive discounting**: Giving too many discounts eats into profit margins and devalues the product.

- **Underpricing products**: Setting prices too low to attract customers can prevent you from covering costs.

- **Taking out multiple loans at once**: Managing multiple debts can lead to overwhelming interest payments.

- **Ignoring vendor payments**: Late payments to vendors can harm relationships and lead to service issues.

- **Over-spending on office space or luxury items**: Spending on non-essentials before the business is stable can drain cash.

- **Avoiding forecasting**: Not planning for future needs leaves you unprepared for changes in demand.

- **Not negotiating with suppliers**: Missing out on cost savings can reduce profit margins.

- **Failing to set aside money for maintenance**: If equipment breaks down, you'll need cash on hand for repairs.

- **Overestimating revenue**: Relying on optimistic forecasts can lead to overspending.

- **Ignoring professional advice**: Not consulting with financial advisors can lead to poor decision-making.

Vinu: That's a pretty comprehensive list. I'll make sure to steer clear of these mistakes. I can see how they could easily get a business into trouble.

Manu: Exactly, Vinu. These activities might seem harmless individually, but over time, they add up and can destabilize a business. Financial discipline helps you avoid these pitfalls.

4. Building a Financial Mindset

Vinu: How do I develop this disciplined mindset? It seems like I need to start thinking differently about money.

Manu: You're right. Developing a financial mindset is key to building discipline. Here's how you can start:

- **Prioritize Long-Term Gains**: Before making a decision, ask if it will benefit the business long-term. For instance, instead of spending on a fancy office, you might invest in product development for future growth.

- **Embrace Delayed Gratification**: Good things come to those who wait! Sometimes, it's worth delaying immediate rewards to achieve bigger goals.

- **Commit to Learning**: Financial discipline grows with knowledge. Read up on business finance, take courses, or seek advice from mentors. The more you know, the easier it is to make sound financial decisions.

Vinu: So, it's about building habits that keep the business focused on sustainable growth, even if it means making tough choices?

Manu: Exactly. Financial discipline is a mindset that values stability over short-term wins. By cultivating this mindset, you'll make decisions that help the business thrive, even when times are tough.

Vinu: Thanks, Manu. I understand now that financial discipline is like building a strong foundation. It keeps the business stable, ready to grow, and prepared for challenges.

Manu: You've got it, Vinu! Financial discipline is the cornerstone of managing business finance. With it, you're prepared to tackle any challenge and make the most of every opportunity. Now that you understand this principle, everything else we discuss will build on this foundation.

Vinu: Perfect. So, where do we go from here?

Manu: Now, its time to jump into **financial statements**. But before that, we have to understand the importance of having a fool proof accounting system. Because, that's the base for accounting system. Shall we?

Vinu: Yes. I'm ready for it!

.

1.2 The Importance of a Fool-Proof Accounting System

Manu: Vinu, let's try to understand why it's so important to have a solid accounting system in place. Without a reliable accounting system, it's like building a house without a foundation. It might hold up for a while, but eventually, things can come crashing down.

Vinu: I've got a basic system set up, but I'm not sure if it's really that robust. Why is a fool-proof accounting system so essential?

Manu: A fool-proof accounting system is essential because it provides accurate, up-to-date financial information. This data is the lifeline of your business. When you have an organized, reliable accounting system, you're in a position to make informed decisions, catch potential issues early, and even spot opportunities for growth.

Vinu: That sounds important. So it's more than just keeping track of money coming in and going out?

Manu: Absolutely. It's about having a complete, accurate view of your business's financial health at any given moment. Here's how a solid accounting system can make a huge difference:

1. Helps You Track Profitability

Manu: One of the biggest benefits is that it helps you clearly track profitability. A good accounting system shows you exactly where your money is coming from and where it's going. With this information, you can see which products or services are driving profits and which ones might be costing more than they're worth.

Vinu: So, I can see which parts of the business are the most profitable and focus on those?

Manu: Exactly! For example, if you offer multiple services, your accounting system should help you break down revenue by service type. This way, you can prioritize the high-margin services and consider ways to improve or cut back on the lower-margin ones.

2. Ensures Compliance with Regulations

Manu: Another crucial aspect is compliance. A well-organized accounting system helps you stay on top of tax obligations and regulatory requirements. It ensures that your financial records are accurate, which can save you from potential fines or penalties.

Vinu: That's a good point. I've always been a bit worried about missing tax deadlines or making mistakes in my filings.

Manu: A reliable system can help with that. It keeps track of all the necessary documents, making it easy to file accurate tax returns and handle audits if they come up. With accurate records, you don't have to scramble at the end of the year or worry about missing something important.

3. Simplifies Cash Flow Management

Manu: Your accounting system is also a critical tool for managing cash flow. It tracks all your income and expenses, giving you a clear picture of your cash position at any moment. This helps you avoid running into cash flow issues and ensures you have the funds available to cover your expenses.

Vinu: That sounds useful. How does it help with cash flow, specifically?

Manu: For instance, if you can see that cash is running low, you might hold off on certain expenses or focus on collecting payments from customers faster. On the flip side, if cash flow is strong, you might decide it's a good time to reinvest in growth. A fool-proof accounting system helps you make these decisions confidently because you're working with real-time data.

4. Improves Financial Planning and Forecasting

Manu: Planning for the future becomes so much easier when you have accurate, detailed financial data. A good accounting system gives you historical information to base your forecasts on. This allows you to set realistic goals, anticipate potential challenges, and create strategies to reach your targets.

Vinu: So, having reliable financial data from my accounting system helps me set and achieve realistic goals?

Manu: Yes! For example, if you're planning for next year, you can look at past sales trends and expenses to make informed projections. You'll be able to budget accurately, anticipate growth, and adjust strategies based on reliable data rather than guesswork.

5. Enhances Decision-Making

Manu: With accurate financial data, you're in a better position to make key business decisions. Whether you're deciding to expand, hire new employees, or launch a new product, your accounting system provides the insights you need to make informed choices.

Vinu: It's almost like having a dashboard for the business. I can make better decisions when I see all the numbers clearly.

Manu: Exactly, Vinu! When you have everything laid out, it's easier to weigh the pros and cons of each decision. You can analyze the costs, predict the outcomes, and avoid risky moves. A strong accounting system is like a reliable advisor, helping you make decisions with confidence.

6. Helps Build Investor and Lender Confidence

Manu: If you ever plan to seek outside investment or a loan, a fool-proof accounting system is essential. Investors and lenders want to see accurate, well-organized financial statements. A solid accounting system ensures that your financial reports are clear, detailed, and accurate.

Vinu: So, having a good system can also make it easier to secure funding?

Manu: Absolutely. When investors or lenders see that your financials are well-organized and reliable, it builds trust. They'll feel more confident in your business, which can lead to better loan terms or more investment opportunities. Your accounting system is often their first impression of your financial responsibility.

7. Helps with Accurate Financial Statements

Manu: Finally, a reliable accounting system is essential for preparing accurate financial statements. These statements are key to understanding the financial health of your business. Without an organized system, financial statements can be riddled with errors, making it hard to see where your business really stands.

Vinu: I see. And I guess this leads directly to our next topic, right?

Manu: You're spot on, Vinu. Once you have a solid accounting system, it's much easier to prepare accurate financial statements. In the next chapter, we'll dive into these statements in detail. You'll learn how to read them, what each one tells you, and how they all fit together to give you a complete picture of your business's financial health.

Vinu: That sounds perfect! I'm ready to learn more about financial statements now that I understand the importance of having a solid accounting foundation.

Manu: Great! A fool-proof accounting system sets the stage for everything we'll discuss next. Let's get into financial statements and see how they can provide insights into every aspect of your business

1.3 Understanding Financial Statements

Vinu: Alright, Manu, you said we should start with financial statements. But honestly, I've looked at my accountant's reports before, and all I see are numbers. What exactly should I be looking for?

Manu: Vinu, Financial statements can look overwhelming at first, but they're actually designed to give you a snapshot of your business's health. There are three main financial statements you need to focus on: the **balance sheet**, the **income statement**, and the **cash flow statement**. Each one tells you something different, and together, they give you a complete picture of your financial position.

Vinu: Okay, I've heard of those. But what's the difference between them?

Manu: Let's break it down. Think of your **balance sheet** as a snapshot of your business's financial position at a particular point in time. It shows what your business owns (**assets**), what it owes (**liabilities**), and what's left over for you—the owner (**equity**).

Vinu: So the balance sheet is like a report card for my business?

Manu: Exactly! It shows how much you've invested and how much your business has borrowed. It's called a "balance" sheet because the equation must always balance: **Assets = Liabilities + Equity**.

Vinu: That makes sense. But how does it help me?

Manu: Your balance sheet helps you understand the financial strength of your business. For instance, it tells you whether your business has enough assets to cover its liabilities. If your liabilities are too high compared to your assets, you might run into trouble paying off debts. It also shows you how much equity you've built in your business, which is important when considering expansion or taking on more debt.

Vinu: Alright, what about the **income statement**? I know it shows profit, but is there more to it?

Manu: The income statement is all about **profitability**. It shows your business's performance over a specific period—usually a month, quarter, or year. The key figures to look at are **revenue**, **expenses**, and **net profit**.

Vinu: So, it's telling me whether I'm making or losing money, right?

Manu: Exactly. But don't stop at the net profit. Look closely at **gross profit** too, which is your revenue minus the cost of goods sold. This helps you understand if your pricing and production costs are aligned. And if your operating expenses are too high, they'll eat into your net profit, so you need to monitor that as well.

Vinu: Got it. So, the income statement shows how well my business is performing over time?

Manu: Yes. It's like checking your business's pulse—if your profits are increasing, your business is healthy. But if your profits are shrinking, you'll need to figure out why.

Vinu: And what about the **cash flow statement**? I've heard it's different from the income statement, but I'm not sure how.

Manu: You're right, the **cash flow statement** is different. While the income statement shows profits, the cash flow statement tells you how much cash is actually moving in and out of your business. Remember, profits don't always mean cash, and you can't pay bills with profits—you need actual cash.

Vinu: That's interesting. So even if I'm showing a profit, my business can still be short on cash?

Manu: Absolutely. That's a common issue for many businesses. The cash flow statement is divided into three sections: **operating activities**, **investing activities**, and **financing activities**. This shows where your cash is coming from and where it's going, whether it's from your day-to-day operations, investments, or loans.

Vinu: So, the cash flow statement helps me see if I have enough cash to keep things running?

Manu: Exactly. It helps you monitor whether your operations are generating enough cash to cover expenses, or if you need to rely on external financing. It's crucial for managing your business's liquidity.

Vinu: This makes things clearer. So, the balance sheet tells me where I stand, the income statement shows me how well I'm performing, and the cash flow statement tells me whether I have enough cash to keep the business running. Is that it?

Manu: That's it in a nutshell! These three financial statements are the foundation of your business's financial health. They help you make decisions like whether you can afford to expand, if you need to cut costs, or whether you should raise more capital.

Vinu: This is starting to make sense. But how often should I be looking at these statements?

Manu: Ideally, you should review them monthly. The more frequently you look at them, the quicker you can spot trends or problems and make adjustments. It's all about being proactive, not reactive.

Case Study:

Vinu: Manu, I'm excited to put everything we've talked about into practice, but I'm still a bit unsure about how these financial statements apply to real situations. Do you have a real-world example to help me understand better?

Manu: Sure, Vinu! Imagine you run a small business that sells electronic gadgets. Let's call it **TechZone**. You've been in business for three years, but recently, your sales have plateaued. Now you're concerned about where your business stands financially and what to do next.

Vinu: Yes, that's exactly my worry. I'm not sure how to address the issue. What's the first step?

Manu: The first step is to analyze your **financial statements** to understand the complete picture. Financial statements include three key reports:

- The **balance sheet** (which shows what your business owns and owes at a specific point in time),

- The **income statement** (which shows your revenue and expenses over a period of time), and

- The **cash flow statement** (which shows how cash is moving in and out of your business).

We'll start with the balance sheet, then move on to the income statement, and finally the cash flow statement. These will help us identify if the business has strong foundations despite the sales plateau and give clues on areas to improve.

Here's a snapshot of **TechZone's balance sheet** as of March 31st, 20X4:

Balance Sheet of TechZone as at 31st March, 20X4

Particulars	Note No:	₹
Equity and Liabilities		
1) Shareholders' funds		
a) Owner's Equity	1	11,00,000
2) Non-current liabilities		
(None)		
3) Current liabilities		
a) Accounts Payable	2	2,50,000
b) Short-Term Loan	3	1,50,000
Total		**15,00,000**
Assets		
1) Non-current assets		
i) Equipment	4	6,00,000
2) Current assets		
i) Inventory	5	4,00,000
ii) Accounts Receivable	6	3,00,000
iii) Cash	7	2,00,000
Total		**15,00,000**

1) Owner's Equity - the amount you would keep after selling all assets and paying all liabilities; it represents your ownership in the business.

2) Accounts Payable - money you owe suppliers for products or services you've already received.

3) Short-Term Loan - a loan you have to repay within one year.

4) Equipment: the value of your equipment like machinery, computers, etc.

5) Inventory - the value of products that you haven't sold yet.

6) Accounts Receivable - money customers owe you for sales you've already made.

7) Cash - money immediately available for use.

Vinu: I see the assets and liabilities, but how does this relate to my concern about sales flattening?

Manu: Good question. Let's break it down.

- **Assets**: These are the resources your business owns that can be turned into cash or used to run the business. Your **inventory** is ₹4,00,000, which is quite significant. If sales are stagnant, this could mean you're holding too much inventory, which ties up cash.

- **Liabilities**: These are the obligations or debts your business must pay. You owe ₹2,50,000 to suppliers (**accounts payable**) and ₹1,50,000 on a **short-term loan**.

- **Equity**: This represents the value left in the business after you've paid off all debts. Your **owner's equity** of ₹11,00,000 shows you own a strong portion of your business, but let's calculate some financial ratios to see if there are any risks.

Let's start by calculating the **current ratio**. This ratio helps us see if your business can cover its short-term liabilities (debts due within one year) with its current assets (cash, inventory, receivables).

- **Current Assets**: These are assets that can be converted into cash within a year, like cash, inventory, and accounts receivable.

- **Current Liabilities**: These are debts you need to pay within a year, like accounts payable and short-term loans.

Here's the formula:

Current Ratio = Current Assets / Current Liabilities

For **TechZone**, we calculate:

- **Current Assets**: ₹2,00,000 (cash) + ₹4,00,000 (inventory) + ₹3,00,000 (accounts receivable) = ₹9,00,000

- **Current Liabilities**: ₹2,50,000 (accounts payable) + ₹1,50,000 (short-term loan) = ₹4,00,000

So, **Current Ratio** = ₹9,00,000 / ₹4,00,000 = 2.25

Vinu: 2.25? So I have more current assets than liabilities. That's good, right?

Manu: Yes, a **current ratio** above 1 means your business has enough assets to cover short-term debts, which is healthy. But because your **inventory** is high, this might mean your sales stagnation is causing a buildup of stock, which ties up cash that could be used elsewhere. Excess inventory is often a sign that products aren't moving as fast as expected.

Vinu: That makes sense. I should look at clearing out old stock. What's the next step?

Manu: Now, let's look at **TechZone's income statement** for the same period. This will help us understand how profitable the business is and how stagnant sales are affecting overall performance:

Income Statement for the year ended March 31st, 2024

Particulars	₹
Revenue	₹ 12,00,000
Less: Cost of Goods Sold (COGS)	₹ 7,00,000
Gross Profit	**₹ 5,00,000**
Less: Operating Expenses	₹ 3,00,000
Operating Profit	₹ 2,00,000
Less: Interest Expenses	₹ 50,000
Net Profit	**₹ 1,50,000**

1) Revenue - the total sales from selling gadgets

2) Cost of Goods Sold (COGS) - the direct costs of making or buying the gadgets you sold

3) Operating Expenses - the costs of running the business, such as salaries, rent, and utilities

4) Interest Expenses - the interest you're paying on loans

5) Net Profit - the profit left after all expenses have been deducted

We can calculate two important ratios to assess your profitability:

1. **Gross Profit Margin:** This shows the percentage of sales left after covering the cost of goods sold (COGS), telling us how efficiently you're producing or sourcing your products.

   - **Gross Profit** = Revenue – COGS = ₹12,00,000 – ₹7,00,000 = ₹5,00,000

   - **Gross Profit Margin** = Gross Profit / Revenue = ₹5,00,000 / ₹12,00,000 = 41.7%

2. **Net Profit Margin**: This shows how much of your sales turn into actual profit after covering all costs, including operating and interest expenses.

   - **Net Profit Margin** = Net Profit / Revenue = ₹1,50,000 / ₹12,00,000 = 12.5%

Vinu: So, 41.7% of my sales are left after covering the cost of goods, and 12.5% of my total revenue turns into profit after all expenses. What does this mean for my business?

Manu: These margins are good, especially for a small business. **A Gross Profit Margin** of 41.7% means that for every ₹100 in sales, ₹41.7 goes toward covering your operating costs. However, with **stagnant sales**, even though your margins are strong, your overall revenue isn't growing. You need to focus on **boosting sales** or **reducing costs** to improve profitability.

Vinu: That's clear. I'm managing costs well, but I need to increase sales. What about the cash flow statement?

Manu: Let's examine **TechZone's cash flow statement** to see how cash is moving in and out of the business:

Cash Flow Statement for the year ended March 31st, 2024

Particulars	₹
Cash Flow from Operating Activities (A)	₹ 3,00,000
Cash Flow from Investing Activities	
Purchase of Equipment	₹ (2,00,000)
Net Cash Flow from Investing Activities (B)	**₹ (2,00,000)**
Cash Flow from Financing Activities	
Proceeds from Short-Term Loan	₹ 50,000
Net Cash Flow from Financing Activities (C)	**₹ 50,000**
Net Increase in Cash & Cash Equivalents (A+B+C)	**₹ 1,50,000**
Cash & Cash Equivalents at the Beginning of the Year	₹25,000
Cash & Cash Equivalents at the End of the Year	**₹1,75,000**

1) Cash Flow from Operating Activities - the cash generated from your core business, like sales and expenses

2) Cash Flow from Investing Activities - the money spent on buying new equipment

3) Cash Flow from Financing Activities - borrowed via a short-term loan

Even though your sales are flat, your **positive cash flow from operations** of ₹3,00,000 indicates that your core business is still generating cash. However, you spent ₹2,00,000 on equipment (investing activities) and took a loan of ₹50,000 (financing activities. Your net cash flow is positive, which means you're generating enough cash to keep operations going.

Vinu: So, even though I spent on equipment, I'm generating enough cash through operations to cover it?

Manu: Exactly! **Positive cash flow from operations** is a healthy sign. However, relying on loans for investment when sales are stagnating could signal that you need to focus on **boosting revenue**. To avoid future financial strain, you should ensure that any borrowing directly supports sales growth or improves cash flow.

Vinu: I see. So while things look stable now, I need to be cautious with my borrowing and focus on sales growth. What's my next move?

Manu: Here's what I suggest:

- **Reduce excess inventory**: Consider offering discounts or promotions to move old stock and free up cash.

- **Increase marketing and sales efforts**: Focus on strategies that will bring in more customers and boost revenue.

- **Monitor cash flow carefully:** Avoid borrowing unless it's necessary to grow sales or improve efficiency.

Vinu: That makes sense!

1.4 Know Your Financial Metrics

Vinu: Manu, now that I've understood the basics of financial statements, I keep hearing about "financial metrics" and how important they are for entrepreneurs. Can you walk me through the key metrics I should be focusing on as a business owner?

Manu: Absolutely, Vinu. **Financial metrics** are essential because they help you measure the financial health and performance of your business. For TechZone, understanding these metrics will guide you in making informed decisions. Let's walk through the most important ones, using TechZone as an example.

A. Gross Profit Margin

Manu: The first one we've already touched on: **Gross Profit Margin**. It's an essential metric because it tells you how much of your revenue is left after covering the **Cost of Goods Sold (COGS)**, which is the direct cost of producing or purchasing the products you're selling.

Vinu: Okay, I think I get that. But why is **Gross Profit Margin** so important?

Manu: Great question. **Gross Profit Margin** is important because it helps you understand how efficiently you're producing or sourcing your products. It tells you how much money you have left after covering the direct costs associated with making your product or delivering your service. Once you know your **Gross Profit**, you can then use that money to cover other expenses like salaries, rent, marketing, and operational costs. The higher your **Gross Profit Margin**, the more efficiently you're managing your production costs.

Let me explain it with **TechZone's** numbers:

Here's the formula:

Gross Profit Margin = (Revenue – COGS) / Revenue

Now, for **TechZone**:

- **Revenue**: ₹12,00,000 (this is the total amount of money you made from selling gadgets)

- **COGS**: ₹7,00,000 (this is what it cost you to produce or purchase those gadgets, including materials, labor, and other direct costs)

Plugging these into the formula:

Gross Profit Margin = (₹12,00,000 – ₹7,00,000) / ₹12,00,000 = 41.7%

This means that for every ₹100 in sales, ₹41.7 is left over after covering the direct costs of making your products. So, that ₹41.7 can be used to pay for your other operating expenses like rent, salaries, and marketing, or reinvested back into the business.

Vinu: I see. So the **Gross Profit Margin** helps me understand how much I have left after covering just the costs of making my products, but before paying for everything else?

Manu: Exactly! That's why **Gross Profit Margin** is often considered a measure of production or sourcing efficiency. It shows how well you're controlling the direct costs of producing your goods or services. If your **COGS** is too high, it'll eat into your margin, leaving you with less money to cover your other expenses.

Vinu: So, if my **Gross Profit Margin** is lower than I'd like, what can I do to improve it?

Manu: There are several ways to improve your **Gross Profit Margin**:

1. Reduce COGS:

This is the most direct way to improve your margin. You can work on negotiating better deals with suppliers, reducing waste in production, or finding more efficient ways to make your products. For example, maybe you can source cheaper materials without compromising quality or optimize the manufacturing process to lower costs.

2. Increase Prices:

If you feel your products are undervalued in the market and can justify a price increase, this is another way to improve your margin. However, you need to be careful with this approach—you don't want to lose customers by raising prices too much.

3. Focus on High-Margin Products:

If some of your products have a higher **Gross Profit Margin** than others, focus on selling more of those. This can improve your overall margin even if your COGS remains the same.

4. Reduce Discounts and Returns:

If you're offering too many discounts or experiencing a lot of returns, it could be cutting into your **Gross Profit Margin**. Review your discounting strategy to ensure it's not harming your profitability.

Vinu: That makes sense. So I can either focus on lowering my direct costs or increasing my prices, depending on what's more feasible for **TechZone**.

Manu: Exactly. Another thing to consider is **benchmarking** your **Gross Profit Margin** against competitors in your industry. For instance, if other companies in your industry have a higher margin, it might indicate that you have room to improve your costs or pricing strategy.

Vinu: Is there a specific number or range I should aim for in terms of **Gross Profit Margin**?

Manu: The ideal **Gross Profit Margin** varies by industry. For example, in manufacturing or retail, a margin of around **30-50%** is generally considered good. In service-based businesses, it can be much higher, often above **70%**, because there are fewer direct costs involved.

For **TechZone**, a **Gross Profit Margin** of **41.7%** is pretty solid, but it's always worth looking for ways to optimize it further, especially if you want to increase profitability in the long run.

Vinu: Got it. So, by keeping my **Gross Profit Margin** healthy, I'm ensuring that I have enough left over to cover my other expenses and still have some profit at the end.

Manu: Exactly. And it also gives you flexibility. A healthy Gross Profit Margin allows you to reinvest in your business, whether that's through marketing, product development, or scaling your operations.

Vinu: Thanks, Manu! So, my **Gross Profit Margin** shows me how well I'm controlling the direct costs of making my gadgets. What's next?

B. Net Profit Margin

Manu: Exactly. The next important metric is the **Net Profit Margin**. While **Gross Profit Margin** shows how much money is left after covering the direct costs of producing your products, **Net Profit Margin** goes one step further. It tells you how much of your total revenue actually turns into **profit** after covering **all expenses**—this includes operating costs, taxes, interest payments, and any other costs your business incurs.

Vinu: So, it's a more comprehensive measure of profitability, right? It includes everything.

Manu: Exactly. **Net Profit Margin** gives you the full picture. It tells you what portion of your sales is actually being converted into **profit** after all the expenses are paid. While **Gross Profit Margin** focuses on efficiency in producing or sourcing products, **Net Profit Margin** focuses on your overall business efficiency. This includes managing costs like rent, salaries, marketing, taxes, and even interest on loans.

Here's the formula:

Net Profit Margin = Net Profit / Revenue

Now, let's apply this to **TechZone**:

- **Net Profit**: ₹1,50,000 (this is your final profit after all expenses, taxes, and interest payments have been accounted for)

- **Revenue**: ₹12,00,000 (this is the total income from selling your gadgets)

Plugging these into the formula:

Net Profit Margin = ₹1,50,000 / ₹12,00,000 = 12.5%

So, a **12.5% Net Profit Margin** means that for every ₹100 in sales, you're keeping ₹12.5 as **actual profit** after all expenses have been deducted.

Vinu: I see. So, while the **Gross Profit Margin** shows how much is left after just covering the costs of making my products, the **Net Profit Margin** tells me how much I'm left with after everything is paid for, including taxes and interest.

Manu: Exactly! That's why **Net Profit Margin** is such a key measure of **overall business profitability**. It's the final number that tells you how much profit your business is generating relative to your total sales. The higher your **Net Profit Margin**, the more efficiently your business is running.

Let's break it down a bit more:

Why is Net Profit Margin Important?

1. Measures Total Profitability:

Net Profit Margin is one of the best indicators of how profitable your business is after all expenses. It tells you how well you're managing **all aspects** of your business, from production costs to administrative expenses, marketing costs, taxes, and interest payments.

2. Helps Identify Cost Issues:

If your **Net Profit Margin** is lower than expected, it's often a sign that your **operating expenses** or **non-operating costs** (like taxes or interest) are too high. By monitoring this margin, you can pinpoint where costs might be getting out of hand and make adjustments.

3. Attracts Investors and Lenders:

A strong **Net Profit Margin** makes your business more attractive to **investors** and **lenders** because it shows that you're not only making sales but also turning those sales into actual profit. Investors want to see that a business can generate healthy profits after covering all its costs.

4. Sustainability and Growth:

If you want to grow your business, your **Net Profit Margin** will give you a clear idea of how much you can reinvest. The higher the margin, the more you can potentially put back into the business to drive further growth.

Vinu: That makes sense. So, if my **Net Profit Margin** is low, it could mean I'm spending too much on things like operating costs, taxes, or interest, even if my **Gross Profit Margin** is high.

Manu: Exactly! That's why both margins are important. You could have a healthy Gross Profit Margin, but if your Net Profit Margin is low, it might mean your non-production expenses are eating into your profits. For example, you could be spending too much on rent, salaries, marketing, or other operational costs.

How Can You Improve Net Profit Margin?

1. Reduce Operating Costs:

If your **Net Profit Margin** is lower than you'd like, the first step is to look at your **operating expenses**. These include rent, utilities, salaries, and other day-to-day costs. Cutting unnecessary costs or improving efficiency in these areas can help boost your **Net Profit Margin**.

2. Manage Taxes Efficiently:

Taxes can be a major drain on profitability. Work with your accountant or financial advisor to ensure you're taking advantage of all available tax deductions, credits, and incentives. Reducing your tax burden can have a significant impact on your **Net Profit Margin**.

3. Lower Interest Payments:

If you're paying high-interest rates on loans, refinancing to lower rates or paying off debt faster can reduce your interest expenses and improve your margin.

4. Increase Revenue Without Increasing Costs Proportionally:

One of the most effective ways to improve your **Net Profit Margin** is to increase your sales **without a corresponding increase in costs**. For example, if you can boost sales through marketing or by entering new markets without significantly increasing your overheads, your profits will increase more than your costs, thus improving your margin.

Vinu: That's really helpful. So, it's not just about cutting costs but also about managing things like taxes, interest, and making sure that my costs don't rise too much as I grow sales.

Manu: Exactly. It's all about **efficiency**. Your goal should be to maximize the gap between your revenue and your total costs, so you end up with a healthy profit at the end of the day. The **Net Profit Margin** is one of the best ways to measure that gap and ensure you're running a profitable business.

Vinu: What would be considered a "good" **Net Profit Margin**?

Manu: The ideal **Net Profit Margin** varies by industry. For example:

- **Service-based businesses** tend to have higher margins because they don't have high production costs. It's not uncommon to see **Net Profit Margins** of **15-25%** or higher in these industries.

- **Retail or manufacturing businesses**, which have higher costs, typically have lower margins, often in the **5-10%**range.

For **TechZone**, a **12.5% Net Profit Margin** is pretty solid. But as with most things in business, there's always room for improvement, especially if you want to increase your profitability and scale.

Vinu: So, if I want to improve **TechZone's Net Profit Margin**, I should look at ways to control costs, manage taxes efficiently, and make sure that my sales growth doesn't lead to a proportionate rise in expenses.

Manu: Exactly, Vinu! By keeping an eye on your **Net Profit Margin**, you'll always know how much of your total sales is turning into actual profit, after everything else has been paid for. It's a critical metric for understanding your business's financial health and profitability.

Vinu: Thanks, Manu! I'm definitely going to start tracking **Net Profit Margin** more closely. It'll help me stay on top of my overall profitability and make better decisions for **TechZone**.

Manu: That's the right approach! Keep monitoring it regularly, and you'll have a clear view of how well your business is performing in terms of profitability.

C. Current Ratio

Manu: Right. Now, let's move to **liquidity**. One of the key liquidity metrics you should be aware of is the **Current Ratio**. It helps you assess whether your business has enough **current assets** to cover its **short-term liabilities**. In simpler terms, it tells you if your business can meet its debts and obligations that are due within the next year.

Vinu: So, it's like a measure of how well I can handle my short-term obligations with the assets I have on hand?

Manu: Exactly! The **Current Ratio** shows how easily your business can convert its current assets—like cash, inventory, and accounts receivable—into cash to pay for its short-term liabilities, such as accounts payable, short-term loans, or any other debts due within a year. This is crucial because liquidity is what keeps your business running day to day.

Here's the formula:

Current Ratio = Current Assets / Current Liabilities

Let's apply this to **TechZone**:

- **Current Assets**: ₹9,00,000 (this includes cash, inventory, and money owed to you by customers, also known as accounts receivable)

- **Current Liabilities**: ₹4,00,000 (this includes money you owe to suppliers, short-term loans, and other debts that are due within a year)

Now, plugging these into the formula:

Current Ratio = ₹9,00,000 / ₹4,00,000 = 2.25

This means that for every ₹1 you owe in short-term liabilities, you have ₹2.25 in current assets. So, a **Current Ratio of 2.25** means you have more than twice the assets needed to cover your short-term obligations.

Vinu: Great! That's reassuring. So as long as this ratio stays above 1, I'm in a good position, right? It means I'm not in immediate danger of running out of cash to pay my bills.

Manu: Exactly. A **Current Ratio** above **1** means that your business is considered **liquid**—you have enough assets on hand to cover your short-term debts. The higher the ratio, the more cushion you have. In your case, with a **Current Ratio of 2.25**, it's a very healthy liquidity position. It means that for every ₹100 of short-term liabilities, you have ₹225 of current assets available to cover them.

However, while a ratio above 1 is good, you don't want it to be **too high** either.

Vinu: Wait, why not? Wouldn't a higher ratio be even better?

Manu: It might seem that way, but if your **Current Ratio** is too high, it could indicate that your business is **not using its assets efficiently**. For example, if you're holding too much cash or too much inventory, it might mean that your money is tied up in unproductive assets instead of being invested back into the business for growth.

Think of it this way:

If your ratio is much higher than industry norms, it might suggest that you're not taking full advantage of opportunities to grow or invest in your business.

On the other hand, a **low ratio** (below 1) means you might struggle to meet your short-term obligations, which could lead to cash flow problems.

It's all about finding the **right balance**.

Vinu: I see. So, a **Current Ratio** that's too high could mean I'm sitting on too much inventory or cash that could otherwise be used to expand or invest in the business?

Manu: Exactly! Ideally, you want a **Current Ratio** that's healthy for your business and your industry. For example, a ratio between **1.5 and 2.5** is usually considered strong, but it can vary depending on your industry. If your ratio is too high, it might be worth looking into ways to put some of your idle assets—like excess cash or slow-moving inventory—to better use, like expanding into new markets or investing in marketing.

Vinu: So, how do I know if my ratio is in the right range?

Manu: A good place to start is by looking at **industry benchmarks**. Different industries have different expectations for liquidity:

For example, retail businesses might operate well with a **Current Ratio** closer to **1.5**, since they tend to turn over inventory and collect receivables more quickly.

Capital-intensive industries like manufacturing might need a **higher Current Ratio** — closer to **2** — because they have larger ongoing operational costs and capital requirements.

Your Current Ratio of 2.25 for TechZone is quite solid, suggesting that you're managing your liquidity well. But it's also important to compare your ratio to similar companies in your industry to get a more accurate sense of how you're performing.

Vinu: Got it. So, I should aim to keep it within that healthy range and make sure I'm not holding on to too many idle assets like inventory or cash that could be put to better use.

Manu: Exactly. One area to monitor closely is your **inventory**. If your inventory is building up and not moving as quickly as it should, it could mean that too much of your cash is tied up in stock. Similarly, if you're holding on to more cash than you need for day-to-day operations, you could consider reinvesting that cash in areas like product development, marketing, or expansion.

Vinu: That's really helpful. But what if my **Current Ratio** drops below 1? What does that mean for **TechZone**?

Manu: If your **Current Ratio** falls below **1,** it means your business might not have enough current assets to meet your short-term obligations. This is a red flag for liquidity, and it suggests that you may face difficulty in paying off your debts as they come due. It could lead to cash flow problems, and you might need to take quick action to improve liquidity, like:

- **Collect receivables faster:** Speed up payments from customers.

- **Reduce inventory**: Clear out excess stock to free up cash.

- **Retain Profits:** Retain and reinvest profits into the business to manage liquidity.

- **Raise long term financing**: You might need to raise a long term fund (Debt or Equity) to manage liquidity position.

Vinu: So, if the ratio drops below 1, it's a sign that I need to act fast to improve liquidity and ensure I don't run into cash flow issues.

Manu: Exactly! Monitoring your **Current Ratio** regularly can give you an early warning system. It helps you spot potential liquidity problems before they become serious. The key is to maintain a ratio that ensures you can comfortably meet your short-term obligations while still using your assets efficiently.

Vinu: Thanks, Manu! I feel much clearer about the **Current Ratio** now. I'll make sure to keep an eye on it and ensure **TechZone** maintains a healthy balance between liquidity and asset utilization.

D. Quick Ratio (Acid Test)

Manu: Yes, Vinu, but let's also check your **Quick Ratio**, which is also known as the **Acid Test Ratio**. This is a more stringent measure of liquidity compared to the **Current Ratio**. It's designed to test how well your business can meet its short-term obligations **without** relying on selling inventory.

Vinu: Wait, why exclude inventory? Isn't inventory a current asset too?

Manu: Good point! The reason we exclude **inventory** from the **Quick Ratio** is that inventory can sometimes take longer to turn into cash compared to other current assets like **cash** or **accounts receivable**. In some cases, inventory may not sell as quickly as expected, or it might not be liquid enough to cover short-term obligations immediately. So, the **Quick Ratio** focuses on the most **liquid** assets that can be quickly converted to cash if needed.

Here's the formula:

Quick Ratio = (Current Assets – Inventory) / Current Liabilities

Let's apply this to **TechZone**:

Particulars	₹
Current Assets	9,00,000
Inventory	4,00,000
Current Liabilities	4,00,000

Current Assets - this includes cash, inventory, and accounts receivable

Inventory - the portion of your current assets tied up in stock

Current Liabilities - your short-term obligations, like supplier payments and short-term loans

Now, plugging these into the formula:

Quick Ratio = (₹9,00,000 – ₹4,00,000) / ₹4,00,000 = 1.25

This means that even if you couldn't sell any of your inventory, you'd still have **1.25 times** the current assets needed to cover your short-term debts. So for every ₹1 in short-term liabilities, you have ₹1.25 available in the form of highly liquid assets, like cash and accounts receivable, to pay them off.

Vinu: That makes sense. So, if sales slow down and I can't move my inventory quickly, the **Quick Ratio** tells me how safe I am without relying on selling stock. But how does it compare to the **Current Ratio**?

Manu: Exactly. While the **Current Ratio** includes inventory, the **Quick Ratio** gives you a more conservative measure of liquidity by excluding it. This is particularly important in businesses where inventory might not turn into cash quickly, or if you're facing a period of slow sales. If your **Quick Ratio** is healthy, it shows that you can still cover your short-term debts without needing to sell your stock immediately.

Let's compare:

- **Current Ratio** for **TechZone** was **2.25**, which means you have ₹2.25 of current assets (including inventory) for every ₹1 of liabilities.

- **Quick Ratio** is **1.25**, which focuses on the most liquid assets, excluding inventory.

Both ratios are above **1**, which is a good sign, but the **Quick Ratio** is more cautious and gives a better picture of how well you can handle immediate cash needs.

Why Is the Quick Ratio Important?

1. More Conservative View of Liquidity:

The **Quick Ratio** provides a more conservative view of your business's liquidity because it only includes assets that can be converted to cash **quickly**. It's especially useful in industries where inventory might not be sold easily or where stock turnover is slow.

2. Helps During Market Downturns or Slow Sales:

If your business experiences a slowdown in sales, you can't always count on selling inventory quickly. In such cases, the **Quick Ratio** helps you see if you have enough highly liquid assets (cash and receivables) to meet your short-term obligations without relying on inventory.

3. More Insight for Lenders and Investors:

Investors and lenders often look at the **Quick Ratio** as an additional measure of financial health. It reassures them that even if your business struggles to sell inventory, you can still meet your debt obligations with the liquid assets you have on hand.

Vinu: I see. So, it's like a **stress test** for liquidity—if things slow down and I can't sell my stock, the **Quick Ratio** tells me if I'm still in a safe position to pay off my short-term liabilities.

Manu: Exactly! It's a way to ensure that you're not relying too heavily on inventory to stay liquid. In industries where inventory is less liquid or takes longer to sell, the **Quick Ratio** can be a better indicator of your ability to meet obligations.

What's a Good Quick Ratio?

A **Quick Ratio** of 1 or higher is generally considered good because it means you have enough liquid assets to cover your short-term liabilities. For **TechZone**, a **Quick Ratio** of **1.25** is healthy—it means you have enough liquid assets on hand to cover your debts even if you can't sell any inventory.

If the **Quick Ratio** falls **below 1**, it could be a sign that your business is too reliant on inventory to meet short-term obligations, which can be risky.

A **Quick Ratio** that is too high (e.g., **2 or higher**) might suggest that your business has too much idle cash or receivables that aren't being put to good use. In that case, you could consider reinvesting some of that cash to fuel growth or expand operations.

Vinu: So, just like with the **Current Ratio**, there's a balance to maintain. A **Quick Ratio** that's too low means I'm relying too much on selling inventory, but if it's too high, it might mean I'm not using my cash or receivables effectively.

Manu: Exactly! You want a **Quick Ratio** that shows you're financially stable, but also that you're making good use of your liquid assets. If your ratio is too low, it might indicate that you could struggle to meet short-term obligations, especially if sales slow down or inventory becomes harder to sell. On the other hand, if it's too high, it might be a sign that you're not using your available cash to grow the business.

How Can You Improve Your Quick Ratio?

1. Convert Non-Quick Assets to Quick Assets: One way to improve your Quick Ratio is by converting non-quick assets (like inventory) into quick assets (cash or receivables). For example, you can have clearance sales to reduce excess inventory and generate cash. This boosts your liquidity since the cash from sales directly contributes to quick assets.

2. Reduce Short-Term Liabilities Strategically: To improve your Quick Ratio, you can reduce unnecessary short-term liabilities. This doesn't mean extending credit terms with suppliers, which would actually increase liabilities; rather, focus on paying off high-interest short-term loans or consolidating debts to improve your financial position without straining cash flow.

3. Increase Cash Reserves:

Building up cash reserves can improve your **Quick Ratio**. This might involve holding back some profits rather than reinvesting everything right away, giving you more flexibility to cover short-term obligations.

4. Control Inventory Levels:

Keeping inventory lean is another way to improve liquidity, even though inventory isn't included in the **Quick Ratio**. By not tying up too much cash in unsold stock, you'll free up more liquid assets to improve your overall financial position.

Vinu: That's really helpful. So, if my **Quick Ratio** is lower than I'd like, I can focus on converting non-quick assets into quick assets, reducing short-term liabilities, building up cash reserves and control inventory levels to strengthen my position.

Manu: Exactly. The **Quick Ratio** is a great way to see how well-positioned your business is to meet short-term obligations without relying on inventory. By keeping an eye on it, you'll be able to react quickly if you notice liquidity tightening, especially in times of slow sales or economic uncertainty.

Vinu: Thanks, Manu! I'll make sure to keep track of the **Quick Ratio** as well. It seems like a great way to ensure I'm not too dependent on inventory for covering short-term obligations.

E. Return on Assets (ROA)

Manu: Exactly. Now, let's talk about **efficiency metrics**, starting with **Return on Assets (ROA).** This metric shows how efficiently your business is using its assets to generate profit. It's especially important for **capital-intensive businesses**—those that require significant investment in assets like machinery, equipment, or real estate.

Vinu: So, **ROA** helps me see if I'm getting good returns from the assets I've invested in, right?

Manu: Exactly! **ROA** is a measure of how well your business is using its **total assets**—both current and non-current—to produce profits. In simple terms, it tells you how much profit you're generating for every ₹100 of assets your business owns. A higher **ROA** indicates that your business is using its assets efficiently, while a lower **ROA** may suggest that your assets aren't being used effectively to drive profit.

Here's the formula:

ROA = Net Profit / Total Assets

Let's look at **TechZone**:

Particulars	₹
Net Profit	1,50,000
Total Assets	15,00,000

Net Profit - this is the profit after all expenses, including taxes, have been paid

Total Assets - this includes everything you own, like cash, inventory, equipment, and property

Now, plugging these into the formula:

ROA = ₹1,50,000 / ₹15,00,000 = 10%

This means that for every ₹100 in assets, you're generating ₹10 in profit. So, an **ROA of 10%** shows that you're getting a decent return from the assets you have in your business.

Vinu: I see. So, **ROA** tells me how efficiently I'm using my assets to generate profit. If I invest in more equipment or assets, I should aim to increase my **ROA** to ensure those assets are producing more profit, right?

Manu: Exactly! A higher **ROA** means you're making better use of the assets you have. If you decide to invest in new equipment, for example, you want to make sure that this investment translates into higher profits. It's not just about acquiring assets—it's about using them effectively to drive growth and returns.

Why is ROA Important?

1. Measures Asset Efficiency:

ROA gives you insight into how well your business is utilizing its assets. If your **ROA** is high, it means your assets are being put to good use to generate profits. A low **ROA**, on the other hand, might indicate that your assets are underutilized or that you're carrying too many unproductive assets.

2. Helps in Decision-Making for Asset Investments:

When you're considering investing in new assets—like equipment, property, or technology—you can use **ROA** to measure whether those investments are actually improving your profitability. Ideally, after acquiring new assets, you want to see your **ROA** increase, indicating that the assets are contributing to the growth of your business.

3. Comparing Across Businesses or Industries:

ROA is also useful for comparing how efficiently different businesses or industries use their assets. For instance, a tech company might have a high **ROA** because it doesn't need many physical assets to generate profit, while a manufacturing company might have a lower ROA due to the capital-intensive nature of the business.

Vinu: So, if I'm planning to invest in more equipment, I should track how it affects my **ROA**. If my **ROA** increases after the investment, it means the assets are being used efficiently, right?

Manu: Exactly. A higher **ROA** after making an investment would indicate that the new assets are helping you generate more profit. It's a great way to ensure that your investments are paying off.

What's a Good ROA?

A "good" **ROA** depends on the industry you're in. In capital-intensive industries, like manufacturing, an **ROA** of **5-15%** is often considered good because these businesses require a lot of assets to generate profit. In less capital-intensive industries, like tech or consulting, where fewer assets are needed, you might expect a higher **ROA**—around **15-20%** or more.

For **TechZone**, an **ROA of 10%** is moderate. However, if you invest in more assets, you'll want to ensure your **ROA** either stays the same or improves to confirm that those new assets are contributing to profitability.

Vinu: That's really helpful. I'll make sure to keep an eye on my **ROA** when I make any new investments. If it drops, that would be a sign that I'm not using my assets as efficiently as I should be, right?

Manu: Exactly! If your **ROA** drops after an investment, it could indicate that the new assets aren't being used effectively or that they're not generating enough profit to justify the investment. In that case, you'd want to dig deeper into why—maybe the equipment isn't being fully utilized, or the new assets aren't driving as much growth as expected.

How Can You Improve Your ROA?

1. Increase Profitability Without Increasing Assets:

The simplest way to improve your **ROA** is to increase profits without adding new assets. You can do this by boosting sales, cutting unnecessary costs, or increasing your margins. The higher your profit relative to your assets, the higher your **ROA** will be.

2. Use Assets More Efficiently:

If your assets aren't being fully utilized, focus on improving their efficiency. For example, if you've invested in new machinery but it's only being used part-time, finding ways to use it more fully can improve your **ROA**.

3. Dispose of Unproductive Assets:

If you have assets that aren't contributing to profitability—such as excess inventory or underused equipment—consider selling or repurposing them. This reduces your total assets and can improve your **ROA** by making your business more efficient.

4. Make Smart Asset Investments:

When investing in new assets, always ask yourself: "Will this help increase profits?" If the answer is yes, then it should improve your **ROA**. However, if you're unsure whether an investment will directly lead to higher profits, it's worth reconsidering or finding a more efficient way to use your existing assets.

Vinu: So, improving my **ROA** is about finding ways to either increase profit or use my assets more efficiently. If I add new assets, I should ensure they're driving enough profit to maintain or improve my **ROA**.

Manu: Exactly. **ROA** is all about efficiency. You want to maximize the returns on the assets you have, whether by increasing profitability or making sure every asset is being used to its full potential. It's a great metric to track regularly, especially when you're making major investment decisions.

Vinu: Thanks, Manu! I'll definitely start paying closer attention to **ROA** when evaluating how well I'm using **TechZone's** assets and when planning new investments.

F. Return on Equity (ROE)

Manu: Now let's talk about **Return on Equity (ROE).** It's one of the most important metrics for measuring how effectively you're using your equity—whether it's your own money or your investors' money—to generate profit.

Vinu: I know it's an important metric, but how exactly does it help me as a business owner?

Manu: Great question. The **ROE** essentially tells you how much **return** you're getting from the money you've invested in the business. It measures the profitability of your company in relation to your **equity**, which is the amount you or your investors have put into the business. In simpler terms, it shows how well your business is using the capital that belongs to the owners.

Here's the formula:

ROE = Net Profit / Owner's Equity

Now, let's use **TechZone** as an example:

- **Net Profit**: ₹1,50,000

- **Owner's Equity**: ₹11,00,000

So, plugging these into the formula:

ROE = ₹1,50,000 / ₹11,00,000 = 13.6%

This means that for every ₹100 of equity you've invested in **TechZone**, you're generating ₹13.6 in profit.

Vinu: I see, so **ROE** tells me how much profit I'm making from my own investment in the business. But why is this important compared to other profitability metrics like Net Profit Margin?

Manu: That's a great observation! While **Net Profit Margin** shows you how much profit you're making from your total sales, **ROE** focuses specifically on how efficiently your equity—your personal or investors' capital—is being used to generate that profit. In other words, it tells you how well you're **leveraging your equity** to create returns.

Here's why it's important:

1. Measures Efficiency of Capital Use:

ROE shows how efficiently the company is using the owners' or shareholders' money to generate profits. If the **ROE** is high, it means the company is doing a good job of using its capital to make profits. If it's low, it might indicate that the company isn't making the most of its equity.

2. Investor Confidence:

If you have outside investors or plan to attract them in the future, **ROE** is something they'll closely watch. Investors want to know how much return they'll get on the money they've invested in your business. A higher **ROE** signals that your business is profitable and effectively using their capital, which makes your company more attractive to investors.

3. Owner's Perspective:

From your perspective, it's about understanding how much profit you're making on your own investment in the business. If your **ROE** is consistently strong, it shows that you're growing your wealth efficiently. However, if it's low, it could mean your business isn't making the most of the money you've put in.

Vinu: That makes sense. So, a higher **ROE** is better because it means I'm getting a better return on the equity I've invested. What would be considered a "good" ROE?

Manu: Yes, a higher **ROE** is generally a good sign. What's considered a "good" **ROE** depends on the industry and the company's stage of growth, but typically, an **ROE** of **15%** or **higher** is considered strong for most businesses. In your case, an **ROE** of **13.6%** is solid, but there's always room for improvement.

However, you need to be cautious—sometimes a high **ROE** can be due to high debt. If a company takes on a lot of debt, it can increase its **ROE** because there's less equity (since debt doesn't count as equity) but potentially more profit. That's why it's important to also monitor your **Debt-to-Equity Ratio** to make sure you're not artificially inflating your **ROE** with too much debt.

Vinu: So, if my **ROE** is rising because I'm borrowing too much, it could give a false sense of profitability, right?

Manu: Exactly! It's important to strike the right balance. A high **ROE** due to efficient use of equity is great, but if it's because of excessive debt, it can become risky in the long run.

Let's say you borrow a lot of money and that increases your profits. That will make your **ROE** look higher because your equity stays the same while profits grow. But if something goes wrong—like a market downturn or a drop in sales—your debt will still be there, and it could put your business in a tough position.

Vinu: Got it. So I need to monitor both **ROE** and my debt levels to ensure I'm not overstretching myself.

Manu: Exactly! Another thing to consider is your **industry's average ROE**. Some industries, like tech or software, tend to have higher **ROEs** because they require less capital to operate. On the other hand, capital-intensive industries, like manufacturing, usually have lower **ROEs** because they need significant investment in machinery, equipment, and other assets.

Vinu: So, comparing my **ROE** to others in my industry helps me see how I'm performing relative to the competition?

Manu: Yes, that's a good benchmark. If your **ROE** is higher than the industry average, it indicates that you're managing your equity well compared to your competitors. If it's lower, it could be a signal that you need to improve your efficiency or profitability.

Vinu: That's really helpful. I'll definitely start keeping a close eye on **ROE** as a measure of how well I'm using my equity. But how can I improve it if I find that it's lower than I'd like?

Manu: There are several ways to improve your **ROE**:

1. Increase Profitability:

By boosting your profits, you can improve your **ROE**. This could mean finding ways to increase revenue, cutting unnecessary costs, or improving efficiency.

2. Optimize Equity Usage:

Sometimes companies can improve **ROE** by using equity more efficiently. For example, if you have excess capital sitting idle, consider investing it in growth opportunities, like expanding product lines or entering new markets.

3. Buy Back Shares:

This is more applicable to larger companies, but buying back shares can reduce the equity base and increase **ROE**. However, this strategy needs careful consideration as it reduces available capital for other investments.

4. Leverage Debt Carefully:

As we discussed earlier, taking on **reasonable amounts of debt** can increase **ROE** as long as the debt is used wisely for growth. Just remember not to overleverage, as it can backfire if your business faces a downturn.

Vinu: That makes sense. So improving **ROE** is about increasing profits and using my equity more effectively, but I need to be careful with how much debt I take on.

Manu: Exactly, Vinu. Keep tracking your **ROE** regularly, and it will help you understand how well your business is utilizing its equity to generate profits. It's a key metric that gives insight into your business's financial health and efficiency, so it's definitely one to watch closely.

Vinu: Thanks, Manu! I feel a lot clearer about **ROE** now. I'll make sure to track it along with my other metrics to get a complete picture of how my business is performing.

What about debt? Are there metrics for that?

G. Debt-to-Equity Ratio

Manu: Yes, Vinu, and that brings us to the **Debt-to-Equity Ratio**. It's a key metric that shows the proportion of debt versus equity you're using to finance your business. This ratio tells you how much of your business is funded by **borrowed money** (debt) compared to **your own capital** (equity).

Vinu: I've heard about this before. Can you explain it more clearly?

Manu: Of course. Here's the formula:

Debt-to-Equity Ratio = Total Debt / Owner's Equity

Let's use **TechZone** as an example:

- **Total Debt (Liabilities)**: ₹4,00,000

- **Owner's Equity**: ₹11,00,000

Now, plugging these into the formula:

Debt-to-Equity Ratio = ₹4,00,000 / ₹11,00,000 = 0.36

This means that for every ₹1 of equity (your own money invested in the business), you have **₹0.36** of debt. A ratio of 0.36 is considered low, which suggests that you're not heavily reliant on borrowing, and your business is largely financed by your own equity. That's generally seen as lower risk.

Vinu: So, this ratio helps me see how much of my business is being funded by debt versus how much is from my own capital. But why does it matter if the ratio is higher or lower?

Manu: Good question. A **lower Debt-to-Equity Ratio** means you're using more of your own money (equity) to finance your business rather than borrowing. This is generally safer because you're not relying too much on debt, which reduces the risk of financial strain if sales decline or expenses rise.

However, if your **Debt-to-Equity Ratio** is **too low,** it could mean you're not leveraging debt enough for growth. **Debt can be a useful tool** to fund expansion or invest in new opportunities, provided you can manage it well. On the flip side, a **high Debt-to-Equity Ratio** means you're relying more on borrowed money, which can be risky if your business faces challenges in generating cash flow to meet debt obligations.

Vinu: So, a **lower ratio** is safer, but it could also mean I'm missing opportunities for growth if I don't borrow enough to invest in my business?

Manu: Exactly. Let's break it down further:

What Does a Low Debt-to-Equity Ratio Mean?

- **Low Debt (e.g., 0.36 for TechZone):** This means your business is mostly funded by equity, meaning it's less risky in terms of debt management. You don't owe much money to external parties, so you don't have to worry as much about interest payments or meeting loan repayments during tough times.

- **Downside:** However, by not using debt, you might be limiting your ability to **scale** the business. Borrowing can help you expand faster, buy new equipment, invest in marketing, or enter new markets.

What Does a High Debt-to-Equity Ratio Mean?

- **High Debt**: On the other hand, if your ratio were something like **4.0,** that would mean for every ₹1 of equity, you're carrying ₹4.0 of debt. That's quite risky because it suggests that your business is heavily reliant on borrowing.

- **Upside:** The upside of having more debt is that you can use it to **grow** faster, without needing to raise additional equity, which could dilute your ownership in the business. In a good market, if the investments funded by debt generate higher returns than the cost of the debt (interest), you could see higher **profits**.

- **Downside:** But the downside is that if your business faces difficulties—like a dip in sales—you might struggle to meet loan repayments. Interest will keep accumulating, and if you can't service the debt, lenders may take legal action, which could put your business at risk.

Vinu: I see. It's all about finding the right balance, then. If I keep the ratio too low, I might not take full advantage of opportunities, but if it's too high, I risk getting into trouble if something goes wrong.

Manu: Exactly. A **balanced Debt-to-Equity Ratio** depends on your industry, business model, and risk tolerance. For most businesses, a ratio between **1.0** and **2.0** is often considered healthy. It means you're using debt strategically to grow the business, but you're not overly dependent on borrowing.

When Should You Consider Increasing Debt?

- **Growth Opportunities:** If you have a strong growth plan and you're confident that borrowing money will generate returns higher than the cost of the loan, then increasing debt might be a good idea.

- **Low Interest Rates:** When interest rates are low, borrowing can be a cheaper way to finance expansion. If the cost of borrowing is lower than the return on investment, it makes sense to use debt as leverage.

- **Cash Flow Stability:** If your cash flow is stable, using debt can help you invest in long-term growth without giving up ownership. But remember, the more debt you take on, the more disciplined you need to be about cash flow management.

When Should You Be Cautious About Increasing Debt?

- **Uncertain Cash Flow:** If your business is experiencing cash flow issues or inconsistent revenue, increasing debt can be risky. It may put pressure on you to meet fixed repayment schedules, which could worsen your financial situation.

- **High-Interest Rates:** If interest rates are high, the cost of borrowing might outweigh the benefits of growth. In such cases, it's better to rely more on equity or internal cash reserves to fund expansion.

- **Economic Downturns:** In uncertain or declining economic conditions, it's best to avoid increasing debt. Businesses facing weak demand or shrinking markets should focus on maintaining liquidity rather than leveraging debt.

Vinu: So, I should look at the market conditions, my cash flow stability, and the growth potential before deciding whether to take on more debt.

Manu: Exactly, Vinu. Debt is a double-edged sword. When used wisely, it can help you grow faster and generate higher returns. But if overused or mismanaged, it can create financial stress. Always weigh the risks and rewards before increasing your debt load.

Vinu: Thanks, Manu! This makes a lot more sense now. I'll keep an eye on my **Debt-to-Equity Ratio** and make sure I'm striking the right balance between debt and equity.

Manu: You've got it! Keep monitoring your ratio and use debt strategically. It's a powerful tool when managed properly.

H. Debt Service Coverage Ratio (DSCR)

Manu: Another critical metric for businesses with debt is the Debt Service Coverage Ratio (DSCR). It's one of the most important indicators for measuring your ability to service debt, meaning it shows whether your business generates enough income to cover its debt payments—both interest and principal.

Vinu: I've heard about DSCR, but I've never fully understood how it's calculated and why it's so important. Can you explain it in more detail?

Manu: Of course! The formula for DSCR is:

DSCR = (Profit After Tax + Interest + Depreciation) / Annual Debt Payments

Let's break this down for **TechZone**:

- **Profit After Tax (PAT):** ₹1,50,000 (this is your net profit after paying all taxes)

- **Interest:** ₹50,000 (the interest on your loan)

- **Depreciation:** ₹60,000 (a non-cash expense reflecting the wear and tear on your assets)

- **Total Annual Debt Payments**: ₹1,00,000 (the total amount you're paying towards your loan, including both interest and principal repayments)

Now, plugging these into the formula:

DSCR = (₹1,50,000 + ₹50,000 + ₹60,000) / ₹1,00,000

DSCR = ₹2,60,000 / ₹1,00,000 = 2.6

A DSCR of 2.6 means you're generating 2.6 times the amount of income needed to cover your debt payments. Essentially, you have more than enough income to comfortably manage your loan repayments.

Vinu: That sounds good. But why do we add back interest and depreciation to the Profit After Tax in the numerator? And why do we only consider Profit After Tax (PAT), not other profits like Profit Before Tax (PBT)?

Manu: Great questions! Let me explain.

Why Interest is Added Back

Interest is added back because it's already part of your debt payments, which are included in the denominator. In other words, we don't want to "double count" interest in the calculation. Since you're paying interest as part of your loan repayment, it's a cost directly tied to servicing your debt. Adding it back ensures we get a clearer picture of how much income you're generating to cover both the interest and principal portions of the debt.

In the formula, you're calculating how much operating income you have left after paying taxes, and you want to see how this income compares to your debt obligations, including interest. If we didn't add back interest, we'd be subtracting it twice—once in the Profit After Tax and again in the debt payments, which would distort the ratio.

Why Depreciation is Added Back

Depreciation is added back because it's a non-cash expense. Depreciation reflects the reduction in value of assets over time (like your equipment wearing out), but it's not an actual cash outflow. You're not physically paying depreciation to anyone, so it doesn't affect your ability to make loan payments.

In TechZone, you recorded ₹60,000 as depreciation. While this reduces your taxable income, it doesn't affect your cash flow. Therefore, adding it back to the numerator gives us a true sense of how much cash is available to cover your debt payments.

Why We Use Profit After Tax (PAT)

Profit After Tax (PAT) is used because it reflects the true earnings that are available for servicing debt, after you've fulfilled all your obligations, including taxes. Taxes are a mandatory cost, and they have to be paid before you can service your debt. So, using Profit Before Tax (PBT) would give an inflated view of how much income you actually have available for loan repayments.

In TechZone, after paying ₹1,50,000 in taxes, that's the income you really have left to manage everything else, including your debt payments. The government always gets its share first, so taxes are already deducted when you calculate PAT. This makes PAT a more realistic measure of your available income for debt service.

Vinu: I see! So, interest is added back because it's already included in the debt payments, and we don't want to count it twice. Depreciation is added back because it's not a cash expense, and Profit After Tax is used because it shows the income left after everything else, including taxes, has been paid.

Manu: Exactly! By using Profit After Tax, adding back interest, and ignoring depreciation, you're getting a clearer picture of the actual cash flow available to meet your debt obligations.

Vinu: So, a DSCR of 2.6 means I'm generating 2.6 times the amount I need to cover my debt payments. The higher the DSCR, the better, right?

Manu: Yes, exactly. A higher DSCR means you have a greater margin of safety to make your debt payments. Lenders typically like to see a DSCR of at least 1.5, which means you have 1.5 times the income needed to cover your debts. A DSCR below 1 means you don't have enough income to cover your debts, which can be risky.

Vinu: So, maintaining a high DSCR not only shows that I'm financially stable but also gives lenders confidence in my ability to repay loans.

Manu: That's right! A strong DSCR indicates that your business generates sufficient cash flow to comfortably service its debt. It also gives you more breathing room in case your revenue dips or expenses increase unexpectedly.

I. EBITDA

Manu: Now let's talk about **EBITDA**—which stands for **Earnings Before Interest, Taxes, Depreciation, and Amortization**. This is a really useful metric because it shows how profitable your core business is **without** taking into account financing costs (like interest on loans), taxes, or non-cash expenses (like depreciation and amortization).

Vinu: I've heard of EBITDA, but I am really curious to know, never really understood why we exclude interest, taxes, depreciation, and amortization. What does that tell me about my business?

Manu: Great question! Let me explain. The idea behind **EBITDA** is that it focuses on the **operational performance** of your business. It strips away the effects of decisions related to financing, taxes, and accounting practices. By doing this, **EBITDA** gives you a clearer picture of how well your core operations are performing, without being influenced by external factors like loan interest or tax rates.

Here's the formula:

EBITDA = Net Profit + Interest + Taxes + Depreciation + Amortization

Let's take **TechZone** as an example:

- **Net Profit:** ₹1,50,000 (this is your profit after all expenses, including interest, taxes, and depreciation)

- **Interest:** ₹50,000 (the cost of borrowing, like interest on loans)

- **Taxes:** ₹45,000 (the amount you paid in taxes)

- **Depreciation:** ₹60,000 (this reflects the reduction in value of your assets over time)

Now, plugging these into the formula:

EBITDA = ₹1,50,000 + ₹50,000 + ₹45,000 + ₹60,000 = ₹3,05,000

So, your EBITDA for TechZone is ₹3,05,000.

Vinu: So, **EBITDA** tells me how well my core business is doing without considering things like interest on loans or taxes. Why is it important to separate these out?

Manu: Exactly! **EBITDA** helps you evaluate the **operational profitability** of your business without the influence of financing decisions or tax strategies. Let's break down why we exclude these specific items:

Why Exclude Interest?

Interest is related to how your business is financed. Some businesses have more debt, while others are more equity-financed. By excluding interest, **EBITDA** focuses purely on how your operations are performing, without being affected by how much debt you've taken on or how much interest you're paying.

Why Exclude Taxes?

Taxes vary depending on the country or region your business operates in, and different businesses have different tax strategies. By excluding taxes, **EBITDA** shows how profitable your business is before the impact of taxes, making it easier to compare with other businesses.

Why Exclude Depreciation and Amortization?

Depreciation and amortization are non-cash expenses. Depreciation accounts for the gradual reduction in value of physical assets (like machinery or equipment), and amortization spreads out the cost of intangible assets (like patents or software) over time. Since these aren't cash outflows, excluding them from **EBITDA** helps you focus on your business's **cash-generating ability**.

Vinu: I see. So **EBITDA** is really about understanding how well my core operations are performing, without the influence of financing, taxes, or accounting decisions like depreciation.

Manu: Exactly. That's why **EBITDA** is particularly helpful for comparing businesses. If you're comparing **TechZone** with another company, looking at EBITDA removes the differences in financing structure, tax environment, or the way each business handles depreciation and amortization. It levels the playing field, so you can focus on operational performance.

When is EBITDA Useful?

1. Comparing Businesses:

If you're comparing **TechZone** to another company, EBITDA allows you to compare how well each company's core operations are doing, without the influence of interest, taxes, or accounting choices. It's particularly useful for investors or potential buyers who want to compare businesses in the same industry.

2. Evaluating Profitability:

EBITDA gives a clear view of how much profit your business generates from its core operations. This is important if you want to focus on improving efficiency, reducing costs, or growing your business, because it shows you how profitable your operations are without the noise of non-operational factors.

3. Understanding Cash Flow Potential:

Since **EBITDA** excludes non-cash expenses like depreciation and amortization, it gives you a sense of your business's ability to generate cash from its operations. This is especially useful when you're considering taking on debt or planning to invest in new projects, as it shows how much cash your core business can generate to service debt or fund growth.

Vinu: That makes sense. So, **EBITDA** shows the true health of my business's operations without worrying about how much I'm paying in interest or taxes, and without being affected by non-cash items like depreciation.

Manu: Exactly! However, one thing to keep in mind is that **EBITDA** doesn't account for **capital expenditures** (money spent on buying or maintaining equipment), so it's not a complete measure of cash flow. It shows your business's potential to generate profit from operations, but it doesn't include the cash outflows for things like buying new equipment or paying off debt.

Vinu: So, while **EBITDA** is great for looking at operational performance, I still need to look at other metrics to get a complete picture of my cash flow, right?

Manu: Exactly. **EBITDA** is just one tool in the toolbox. It's great for understanding how profitable your core business is, but to get the full picture of your business's financial health, you'll also want to look at things like **cash flow, capital expenditures**, and **net income** after all expenses, including interest, taxes, and depreciation.

How Can You Improve EBITDA?

1. Increase Revenue:

One of the easiest ways to improve **EBITDA** is to grow your **sales**. More revenue means more profit from operations, which will directly increase your **EBITDA**.

2. Cut Operating Costs:

Another way to improve **EBITDA** is by **reducing operating expenses**. This includes cutting down on costs like salaries, rent, or other overhead expenses that aren't directly tied to production. The more you can reduce these costs, the more profitable your core business will be.

3. Increase Operational Efficiency:

You can also boost **EBITDA** by improving **efficiency** in your operations. For example, if you can produce the same amount of goods with fewer resources or optimize your processes, you'll see an improvement in your **EBITDA**.

Vinu: That's really helpful. So, if I want to improve **TechZone's EBITDA**, I should focus on either increasing sales or cutting down on operating expenses to make the core business more profitable.

Manu: Exactly. The goal is to focus on your **operational performance**— how efficiently and profitably your business is running day-to-day. By keeping an eye on **EBITDA**, you'll have a clear view of how well your core business is doing, and you'll be able to make better decisions on where to improve.

Vinu: Thanks, Manu! I'll definitely start tracking **EBITDA** as a key measure of **TechZone's** operational performance. It seems like a great way to understand how well my business is running at its core.

J. Operating Profit Margin (EBIT Margin)

Manu: Now, let's talk about the **Operating Profit Margin**, also known as the **EBIT Margin**. This metric measures how much of your revenue is left after covering your **operating costs**, but before paying interest and taxes.

Vinu: So, it's different from **Net Profit Margin** because it doesn't consider interest and taxes yet, right?

Manu: Exactly! While **Net Profit Margin** accounts for everything—interest, taxes, and all other expenses—the **Operating Profit Margin** focuses specifically on how much profit you're making from your **core operations,** without factoring in financing costs (like interest) or the impact of taxes. It's a good way to assess how efficiently your business is being run on a day-to-day basis.

Here's the formula:

Operating Profit Margin = Operating Income (EBIT) / Revenue

Let's apply this to **TechZone**:

- **Operating Income (EBIT):** ₹2,10,000 (this is your profit after covering operating expenses like salaries, rent, utilities, and other day-to-day costs, but before accounting for interest and taxes)

- **Revenue:** ₹12,00,000 (this is your total sales or income from selling gadgets)

Now, plugging these into the formula:

Operating Profit Margin = ₹2,10,000 / ₹12,00,000 = 17.5%

This means that for every ₹100 in sales, **₹17.50** is left after you've covered your operating costs. So, an **Operating Profit Margin of 17.5%** means that

17.5% of your revenue is available to cover interest, taxes, and eventually contribute to your **net profit**.

Vinu: I see. So, this metric focuses on how well I'm controlling my **operating expenses** and tells me what portion of my revenue is left over after those costs. It helps me understand how efficiently I'm running the business without looking at interest and taxes yet.

Manu: Exactly! It's a great way to evaluate the **profitability** of your core operations. It shows how well you're managing your day-to-day costs relative to your revenue. If your **Operating Profit Margin** is healthy, it means your business is generating a good amount of profit from its core activities, which gives you more flexibility when it comes to managing interest payments, taxes, and other non-operational expenses.

Why is Operating Profit Margin Important?

1. Measures Operational Efficiency:

Operating Profit Margin tells you how efficiently you're converting revenue into profit after covering operating expenses. If this margin is high, it means you're running your business efficiently, keeping costs under control while generating revenue.

2. Helps Identify Cost Issues:

If your **Operating Profit Margin** is lower than expected, it's a signal that your operating costs might be too high. By tracking this metric, you can identify areas where you might be overspending and take steps to improve efficiency, like reducing unnecessary expenses or negotiating better terms with suppliers.

3. A Focus on Core Operations:

Since **Operating Profit Margin** focuses on the profitability of your core business, it gives you a clear view of how well your core operations are performing. It excludes interest and taxes, which can vary depending on financing decisions or tax policies, so it's a more direct measure of how well your business is running on a daily basis.

Vinu: That makes sense. So, a high **Operating Profit Margin** means I'm doing a good job of keeping my operating costs low relative to my revenue. But what would be considered a "good" **Operating Profit Margin**?

Manu: The ideal **Operating Profit Margin** can vary depending on your industry. For example:

In industries with low operating costs, like software or consulting, you might expect to see **Operating Profit Margins** of **20-40%** or higher.

In more capital-intensive industries like manufacturing or retail, **Operating Profit Margins** are often lower, around **5-15%.**

For **TechZone**, an **Operating Profit Margin of 17.5%** is quite solid, especially in retail where margins tend to be tighter. It shows that you're managing your operational expenses well and keeping a good portion of your revenue as profit.

Vinu: Got it. So, what steps can I take to improve my **Operating Profit Margin** if I find it's lower than I'd like?

Manu: There are a few ways you can improve your Operating Profit Margin:

How to Improve Operating Profit Margin

1. Increase Revenue Without Increasing Costs:

One of the best ways to improve your **Operating Profit Margin** is to grow your revenue **without increasing operating costs proportionally**. For example, you could boost sales through better marketing or entering new markets, while keeping your existing operating expenses the same. This increases the gap between your revenue and your costs, improving your margin.

2. Reduce Operating Costs:

Another way is to **cut unnecessary operating expenses**. This could include renegotiating contracts with suppliers, finding cheaper alternatives for day-to-day costs, or improving operational efficiency (like reducing waste in the production process). The lower your operating costs, the higher your margin will be.

3. Improve Pricing Strategies:

Increasing your prices (without significantly impacting sales) can also improve your **Operating Profit Margin**. If you can raise prices while keeping costs the same, you'll increase the profit you're making from each sale.

4. Control Fixed and Variable Costs:

It's important to monitor both **fixed costs** (like rent and salaries) and **variable costs** (like raw materials). Look for ways to keep fixed costs under control by not expanding too quickly, and try to reduce variable costs by optimizing your supply chain or finding cost-effective production methods.

Vinu: That's really helpful. So, by either increasing revenue or reducing operating costs, I can improve my **Operating Profit Margin** and make **TechZone** more profitable overall.

Manu: Exactly! The key is finding the right balance between growing your revenue and keeping your operating costs under control. By keeping an eye on your **Operating Profit Margin**, you can see how well your core business is performing and make informed decisions to improve efficiency and profitability.

Vinu: Thanks, Manu! I'll make sure to track **Operating Profit Margin** more closely and work on improving efficiency to get the most out of **TechZone's** operations.

K. Debtors Collection Period (DCP)

Manu: Now, let's look at the **Debtors Collection Period (DCP)**, which measures how quickly you're collecting payments from your customers. This metric is crucial for managing your cash flow because it tells you how long it takes for your customers to pay their bills after you've made a sale on credit.

Vinu: So, it's about how long my money is tied up in **accounts receivable** before it actually turns into cash, right?

Manu: Exactly! **DCP** helps you understand the average number of days it takes to collect payments from your customers after a sale. A shorter **DCP** means you're collecting payments quickly, which is good for cash flow. A longer **DCP** means customers are taking longer to pay, which could put a strain on your business's cash flow.

Here's the formula:

DCP = (Average Receivable / Total Credit Sales) * Number of Days

Let's apply this to **TechZone**:

- **Average Receivable**: ₹3,00,000 (this is the total amount customers owe you for sales made on credit)

- **Credit Sales**: ₹12,00,000 (the total sales made on credit, not including cash sales)

Now, plugging these into the formula:

DCP = (₹3,00,000 / ₹12,00,000) * 365 = 91 days

This means that, on average, it's taking you **91 days**—or about **three months**—to collect payments from your customers. That's a long time to wait for cash to come in, which might indicate that you need to tighten your credit terms or encourage faster payments.

Vinu: So, a **91-day DCP** means my customers are taking three months to pay me. Is that bad?

Manu: It depends on your industry, but generally speaking, waiting **three months** to collect payments can be a long time. The longer your **DCP**, the more money is tied up in **accounts receivable**, which means less cash available for running day-to-day operations, paying suppliers, or investing in growth. A shorter **DCP** would improve your **cash flow** because you'd be getting paid faster.

Why is Debtors Collection Period Important?

1. Cash Flow Management:

The **DCP** directly impacts your cash flow. If you're waiting a long time to get paid, it means you're running your business with less cash on hand. This can make it harder to cover operating expenses, pay suppliers, or take advantage of new opportunities because your cash is tied up in unpaid invoices.

2. Helps Identify Payment Issues:

A high **DCP** could indicate that you're offering too generous payment terms, or that some customers are taking advantage of longer credit periods. It can also signal potential collection issues, meaning some customers might be at risk of defaulting or delaying payment beyond what's reasonable.

3. Influences Working Capital:

The longer your **DCP**, the more working capital you need to finance day-to-day operations. If you can shorten your **DCP**, you free up more working capital, which can be used to grow the business or reduce the need for external financing.

Vinu: I see. So, if my **DCP** is high, it might mean I'm giving customers too much time to pay, or they're taking advantage of my payment terms. But if I reduce my **DCP**, I'll improve my cash flow because I'll get paid faster, right?

Manu: Exactly! A shorter **DCP** means you're converting sales into cash faster, which improves liquidity and reduces the pressure on your working capital. By reducing the number of days customers take to pay, you'll have more cash on hand to reinvest in the business, pay off debts, or cover other expenses without having to rely on external funding.

How to Reduce Your Debtors Collection Period

1. Tighten Credit Terms:

One of the simplest ways to reduce your **DCP** is to offer **shorter payment terms**. For example, if you currently give customers **90 days** to pay, you could reduce this to **30 or 45 days**. Shorter payment terms encourage customers to pay sooner and help you get cash into the business faster.

2. Offer Discounts for Early Payments:

Another effective strategy is to offer **early payment discounts**. For example, you could offer a **2% discount** if the customer pays within 10 days. This incentivizes customers to pay quickly in exchange for a small discount, which helps improve your cash flow.

3. Improve Invoice Management:

Make sure you're sending out **invoices promptly** and **following up** with customers regularly. Delays in sending invoices or poor communication can lead to longer payment cycles. Consider automating your invoicing system to ensure that invoices go out as soon as sales are made and set up reminders for overdue payments.

4. Assess Creditworthiness of Customers:

If you're experiencing long **DCP** from certain customers, it may be worth **reassessing their creditworthiness**. Customers who consistently delay payments may not be reliable, and you might need to either tighten credit terms for them or even require **prepayments** in certain cases.

5. Follow Up on Overdue Payments:

Make sure to stay on top of overdue payments. You can set up a system to automatically follow up with customers when payments are due or past due. Being proactive in reminding customers can significantly reduce your **DCP**.

Vinu: Those are really useful tips. So, by tightening credit terms and offering discounts for early payments, I can encourage my customers to pay faster. But how do I know what's an ideal **DCP** for **TechZone**?

Manu: Great question! The ideal **DCP** varies by industry, but generally, a **DCP** of **30 to 60 days** is considered healthy. For retail or fast-moving consumer goods (FMCG), a shorter **DCP**—closer to **30 days**—is typical, since products are sold quickly and payments should follow soon after. In industries with longer sales cycles, such as construction or manufacturing, **60-90 days** might be more common. For **TechZone**, a **DCP** closer to **30-45 days** would be ideal.

Vinu: So, aiming for a **DCP** of **30 to 45 days** would mean I'm getting paid faster, improving cash flow, and reducing the risk of payment issues?

Manu: Exactly. A shorter **DCP** helps ensure that your business has consistent cash flow, which is crucial for running day-to-day operations and fueling growth. The quicker you collect payments, the more cash you have available to invest in the business or pay off expenses.

The Impact of a Long Debtors Collection Period

If your **DCP** remains high (like the current **91 days** for **TechZone**), it could lead to several issues:

- **Cash Flow Shortages:** With money tied up in unpaid invoices, you might struggle to pay suppliers or meet other short-term obligations.

- **Higher Financing Costs:** To cover operating expenses while waiting for customer payments, you may need to rely on external financing (like loans or credit lines), which comes with interest costs.

- **Potential Bad Debts:** The longer an invoice remains unpaid, the greater the risk that it might never be paid, which could lead to **bad debts** and losses for your business.

Vinu: That makes a lot of sense. I'll focus on shortening my **DCP** to improve cash flow and reduce the risk of bad debts. Thanks, Manu!

Manu: You're welcome, Vinu! By managing your **DCP** effectively, you'll have better control over your cash flow and be in a stronger financial position to grow **TechZone**. Keep an eye on it regularly, and make adjustments as needed.

L. Inventory Holding Period (IHP)

Manu: Next, we have the **Inventory Holding Period (IHP),** which measures how long it takes for your inventory to turn into sales. This metric is crucial because it tells you how efficiently you're managing your stock. A high **IHP** means that you're holding onto inventory for too long, which can tie up cash and increase storage costs.

Vinu: So, the longer my **IHP**, the more cash I have tied up in inventory that's just sitting there, right?

Manu: Exactly! Inventory sitting on your shelves or in storage represents **money that isn't being put to use**. A longer **Inventory Holding Period** means you're not selling your products quickly enough, which can hurt your cash flow. Ideally, you want to turn over inventory as fast as possible, so that cash is freed up for other parts of your business—whether that's covering operating expenses or investing in growth.

Here's the formula:

IHP = (Average Inventory / COGS) * Number of Days

Let's apply this to **TechZone**:

Particulars	₹
Average Inventory	4,00,000
COGS (Cost of Goods Sold)	7,00,000

Average Inventory - the value of your stock that's sitting in your warehouse

COGS (Cost of Goods Sold) - the direct costs associated with producing or purchasing the products you sell

Now, plugging these into the formula:

IHP = (₹4,00,000 / ₹7,00,000) * 365 = 208.6 days

This means that, on average, it takes **209 days** for your inventory to be sold. In other words, it takes almost **seven months** to turn your stock into sales, which might indicate that your inventory is moving **too slowly**.

Vinu: Wow, that's a long time! So, if my **IHP** is high like this, it means I need to figure out how to sell my products faster to avoid cash being tied up in inventory for so long.

Manu: Exactly. A high **Inventory Holding Period** means that your products are sitting unsold for an extended period, which ties up cash and can increase costs, such as storage fees or even the risk of products becoming outdated. **Reducing your IHP** would improve your cash flow and free up resources for other uses.

Why is Inventory Holding Period Important?

1. Impact on Cash Flow:

A long **IHP** ties up cash that could be used elsewhere. The longer it takes to sell your inventory, the longer you have to wait to receive cash from those sales. This can create liquidity issues, especially if you have other expenses to cover like rent, salaries, or supplier payments.

2. Indicates Inventory Management Efficiency:

A high **IHP** could mean that you're either **overstocking** or that your products are not selling quickly enough. This might indicate inefficiencies in your inventory management, such as ordering too much stock or not responding quickly to changes in customer demand.

3. Risk of Obsolescence or Spoilage:

If your inventory takes too long to sell, there's a risk that products could become obsolete or lose value over time. For example, in industries like technology or fashion, products can become outdated quickly, leading to markdowns or losses. In other industries, like food or pharmaceuticals, slow-moving inventory might spoil.

Vinu: I see. So, not only is a high **IHP** bad for cash flow, but it also means I might be holding onto stock that could become outdated or lose value if I don't sell it fast enough.

Manu: Exactly! That's why it's crucial to keep your **IHP** as low as possible. The faster you can turn your inventory into sales, the healthier your cash flow will be, and the less risk you'll have of products becoming obsolete or sitting idle for too long.

How Can You Reduce Your Inventory Holding Period?

1. Improve Inventory Forecasting:

One of the most effective ways to reduce your **IHP** is by improving your inventory forecasting. This means predicting demand more accurately so you only stock what you need. You can use sales data, market trends, and seasonality to forecast how much stock you'll need and avoid over-ordering.

2. Run Promotions and Discounts:

If you find that certain products are moving slowly, consider running promotions, offering discounts, or bundling products together to increase sales. These tactics can help clear out old inventory faster and free up cash.

3. Optimize Stock Levels:

Regularly review your stock levels to ensure you're not overstocking. Consider using inventory management software to keep track of how quickly products are selling and to reorder only when necessary. By optimizing your stock levels, you can reduce the time inventory spends sitting on your shelves.

4. Diversify Your Product Offering:

If certain products are consistently moving slowly, it might be time to review your product mix. Introducing new products or discontinuing slow-moving items can help reduce your IHP. Focus on stocking items that have a higher turnover rate.

5. Use Just-In-Time (JIT) Inventory:

The **Just-In-Time** inventory system allows you to minimize the amount of inventory you hold by only ordering stock when you need it. This can significantly reduce your **IHP** by ensuring that you're not sitting on large amounts of unsold inventory.

Vinu: Those are great strategies. So, by improving forecasting, running promotions, and optimizing stock levels, I can move my inventory faster and reduce the amount of cash tied up in it.

Manu: Exactly. The goal is to keep your inventory turnover high, meaning you're selling products quickly and efficiently. The faster you sell, the quicker you get cash into your business, which improves cash flow and reduces the risks associated with holding inventory for too long.

What's a Good Inventory Holding Period?

The ideal **Inventory Holding Period** varies by industry. For example:

- In **retail** or **fast-moving consumer goods (FMCG)**, a low **IHP** is crucial since products need to sell quickly. An **IHP** of **30-60 days** might be typical.

- In **manufacturing** or industries where products are more capital-intensive, an **IHP** of **60-90 days** are most commonly seen.

For **TechZone**, a **209-day IHP** is quite high, indicating that your inventory is moving too slowly. Ideally, you should aim for an **IHP** closer to **90 days** or less, depending on the nature of your products.

Vinu: That makes sense. So, I should aim to reduce my **IHP** to free up cash faster and avoid inventory sitting idle for too long.

Manu: Exactly. By lowering your **IHP**, you'll improve cash flow and reduce the risks associated with holding onto unsold inventory. Monitor your **IHP** regularly, and make adjustments to your inventory management strategy to ensure that you're turning over stock as quickly as possible.

Vinu: Thanks, Manu! I'll start focusing on ways to reduce my **IHP** and improve my inventory management. It seems like a great way to improve cash flow and reduce unnecessary risks.

M. Creditors Payment Period (CPP)

Manu: Another important metric to keep track of is the **Creditors Payment Period (CPP)**, also known as **Days Payable Outstanding (DPO).** This metric measures how long it takes you to pay your suppliers. A higher **CPP** means you're taking longer to settle your debts with suppliers, which can help preserve your cash flow in the short term, but you also need to manage this carefully to maintain good relationships with them.

Vinu: So, a high **CPP** helps me hold on to cash for longer, but if I take too long to pay, my suppliers might get unhappy, right?

Manu: Exactly! While taking longer to pay can improve your **liquidity**, it's important to find a balance. You want to keep your cash flow healthy, but you also need to pay your suppliers on time to maintain good relationships and avoid any disruptions in your supply chain.

Here's the formula:

CPP = (Average Accounts Payable / COGS) * Number of Days

Let's apply this to **TechZone**:

- **Average Accounts Payable**: ₹2,50,000 (the amount you owe to suppliers for goods or services received)

- **COGS (Cost of Goods Sold):** ₹7,00,000 (the cost of producing or purchasing the goods you sell)

Now, plugging these into the formula:

CPP = (₹2,50,000 / ₹7,00,000) * 365 = 130.36 days

This means that, on average, you're taking about **130 days**—or just over **four months**—to pay your suppliers. This could be acceptable if your suppliers are okay with these terms, but you'll want to make sure that you're not taking too long and risking your relationships with them.

Vinu: 130 days sounds like a long time to wait before paying my suppliers. Is that okay, or should I aim to reduce it?

Manu: It depends on your relationship with your suppliers and the industry norms. A **130-day CPP** means you're holding onto cash for longer, which can be good for your cash flow, but it's a long time. You should check whether this is in line with your suppliers' expectations. Some suppliers might be fine with it, especially if they value your business, but others might prefer shorter payment terms.

Why is Creditors Payment Period Important?

1. Helps Preserve Cash Flow:

A longer **CPP** means you're delaying payments to suppliers, which helps you keep cash in the business for longer. This can be helpful if you need to cover other expenses or invest in growth before making payments to suppliers. By delaying payments, you're essentially borrowing from your suppliers interest-free, which can help with liquidity.

2. Supplier Relationships:

However, if your **CPP** is too long, you risk damaging your relationships with suppliers. If suppliers are unhappy with how long you take to pay, they might increase prices, offer you less favorable terms, or even refuse to do business with you in the future. This could disrupt your supply chain and make it harder to run your business smoothly.

3. Industry Norms:

It's also important to compare your **CPP** to industry norms. In some industries, a **90-day CPP** might be standard, while in others, suppliers expect to be paid within **30 to 60 days**. A **130-day CPP** might be too long in certain industries, so understanding what's typical in your sector can help you strike the right balance.

Vinu: I see. So, while it's beneficial to delay payments and hold onto cash, I need to be careful not to strain my supplier relationships by taking too long. How do I figure out the right balance?

Manu: That's exactly right, Vinu! You need to balance keeping your cash flow healthy with maintaining strong relationships with your suppliers. Here's how you can strike that balance:

How to Manage Your Creditors Payment Period Effectively

1. Understand Supplier Terms:

The first step is to understand your suppliers' payment terms. If they offer **30-day, 60-day, or 90-day** payment terms, try to stick within those limits. If you're regularly exceeding the agreed terms, it could strain the relationship. You can also negotiate extended terms if you need more time, but it's important to communicate openly with your suppliers.

2. Use the Time Wisely:

If you're taking longer to pay, make sure you're using that time wisely. For example, if you're delaying payments, use the cash you're holding onto to invest in areas that will generate revenue, like marketing, production, or improving operations. This way, the extra time isn't just about holding onto cash, but using it to grow the business.

3. Negotiate Better Terms:

If you're finding that a **130-day CPP** is stretching your supplier relationships, try negotiating for better terms. You might be able to get **discounts for early payments** or extended credit terms, especially if you have a good relationship with your suppliers. For example, some suppliers might offer a **2% discount** if you pay within 10 days.

4. Maintain Communication:

Keep open communication with your suppliers. If you foresee delays in payments, let them know in advance. Suppliers are more likely to be flexible if you maintain a good relationship and communicate your needs clearly.

5. Track and Monitor Regularly:

Keep an eye on your **CPP** regularly. If it starts creeping up too high, it might be a sign that your cash flow is under pressure. On the other hand, if it's too low, you might be paying suppliers too quickly and missing out on opportunities to better manage your cash flow.

Vinu: That makes sense. So, if my **CPP** is too high, I might risk upsetting my suppliers. But if I reduce it too much, I might be missing out on opportunities to improve my cash flow. It's all about finding the right balance.

Manu: Exactly! Managing your **CPP** well is a balancing act. You want to take advantage of the time you have to hold onto cash and manage liquidity, but you also need to pay your suppliers on time to maintain good relationships. The key is to find that sweet spot where you're optimizing cash flow and keeping your suppliers happy.

What's a Good Creditors Payment Period?

A good **CPP** varies by industry and supplier expectations. For example:

- In industries where suppliers expect quicker payments, like retail or food service, a **CPP** of **30 to 60 days** might be the norm.

- In capital-intensive industries, like manufacturing, a **CPP** of **45 -90 days** could be more common.

For **TechZone**, a **CPP** of **130 days** is quite long, so you might want to assess whether this is aligned with your suppliers' expectations. You can consider reducing it to **90 days** or less to ensure you're not straining supplier relationships.

Vinu: Got it. So, while holding onto cash longer helps with liquidity, I need to ensure that **130 days** isn't too long and that my suppliers are comfortable with these payment terms.

Manu: Exactly. Keep an eye on how your suppliers respond. If they seem comfortable with a longer payment period, it might work in your favor. But if you notice any tension or pushback from them, it's a sign that you may need to reduce your **CPP** to maintain good relationships.

Vinu: Thanks, Manu! I'll make sure to track my **CPP** and talk to my suppliers to ensure that I'm not pushing the limits while keeping cash flow healthy.

N. Cash Conversion Cycle (CCC)

Manu: Now let's talk about the **Cash Conversion Cycle (CCC).** This is a crucial metric that ties together your **Debtors Collection Period (DCP), Inventory Holding Period (IHP),** and **Creditors Payment Period (CPP)** to measure how long it takes for your business to convert investments in inventory and sales into cash. In simple terms, it shows how long your cash is tied up in the entire cycle—from purchasing inventory to selling it and then collecting payment.

Vinu: So, it's about understanding how quickly I can turn the money I've spent on inventory into cash again, right?

Manu: Exactly! A **shorter CCC** means you're more efficient at turning your inventory and receivables into cash, which improves your cash flow. On the other hand, a **longer CCC** means you're waiting longer to convert your investments into cash, which could strain your liquidity.

Here's the formula:

CCC = IHP + DCP – CPP

Let's break this down using **TechZone** as an example:

- **IHP (Inventory Holding Period):** 208.6 days (this is how long it takes for your inventory to be sold)

- **DCP (Debtors Collection Period):** 91 days (this is how long it takes you to collect payments from customers after a sale)

- **CPP (Creditors Payment Period):** 130.36 days (this is how long it takes you to pay your suppliers)

Now, plugging these into the formula:

CCC = 208.6 + 91 – 130.36 = 169.24 days

This means that, on average, it takes **169 days** for **TechZone** to convert its investment in inventory and receivables into cash. So, from the time you buy inventory, sell it, and collect payments from customers, it takes almost **six months** for that cycle to complete.

Vinu: That seems like a long time! So, the **Cash Conversion Cycle** is the total time my cash is tied up in the process of buying inventory, selling it, and then collecting the money?

Manu: Exactly! The **CCC** measures the entire process. A **169-day CCC** means that your cash is tied up for about six months before you fully get it back. A **shorter CCC** would mean that you're moving through this cycle faster—buying inventory, selling it, and collecting payments more quickly—which frees up cash for other uses in the business.

Why is the Cash Conversion Cycle Important?

1. Cash Flow Management:

The **CCC** directly affects your business's cash flow. A shorter **CCC** means you're able to convert your investments in inventory and sales into cash faster, which improves liquidity. This is especially important for small and medium-sized businesses, where cash flow is crucial for day-to-day operations.

2. Efficiency in Operations:

A **shorter CCC** indicates that your business is running efficiently. You're selling inventory quickly, collecting payments from customers promptly, and managing your payment terms with suppliers effectively. A longer **CCC**, on the other hand, might indicate inefficiencies in one or more areas, such as holding onto inventory for too long or taking too long to collect payments.

3. Impact on Growth and Liquidity:

If your **CCC** is long, it means that cash is tied up in the business for an extended period, which can limit your ability to invest in growth, pay off debt, or respond to unexpected expenses. By improving your **CCC**, you'll have more cash available to reinvest in the business, which can fuel faster growth.

Vinu: So, the longer the **CCC**, the more cash is tied up, and I have less flexibility to use that cash for other things, like growing the business or paying expenses?

Manu: Exactly. A long **CCC** means your cash is essentially "stuck" in the process. Improving your **CCC** by reducing your **IHP** (moving inventory faster), shortening your **DCP** (getting paid quicker), or managing your **CPP** (taking longer to pay suppliers when appropriate) can help free up cash and improve liquidity.

How Can You Improve Your Cash Conversion Cycle?

1. Reduce Inventory Holding Period (IHP):

The first way to improve your **CCC** is by reducing your **Inventory Holding Period**. This means selling your inventory faster, which frees up cash sooner. You can do this by improving inventory management, running promotions to clear out stock, or reducing overstocking. The faster you turn inventory into sales, the shorter your **CCC** will be.

2. Shorten Debtors Collection Period (DCP):

Another way to improve your **CCC** is by reducing your **Debtors Collection Period**. This means collecting payments from customers faster. You can achieve this by tightening credit terms, offering discounts for early payments, or improving your invoicing and collection processes. The faster you collect from customers, the quicker you'll have cash in hand.

3. Optimize Creditors Payment Period (CPP):

Finally, you can extend your **Creditors Payment Period**, if possible, without damaging supplier relationships. By taking longer to pay your suppliers, you're holding onto cash for a longer period, which improves liquidity. However, this needs to be managed carefully so you don't strain relationships with suppliers.

Vinu: That makes sense. So, by selling inventory faster, collecting payments quicker, and managing when I pay suppliers, I can reduce my **CCC** and improve my cash flow.

Manu: Exactly.

What's a Good Cash Conversion Cycle?

A "good" **CCC** depends on your industry:

- In **retail** or **FMCG**, where inventory turns over quickly, a **CCC** of **30-60 days** might be ideal.

- In industries like **manufacturing**, where products take longer to produce and sell, a **CCC** of **90-120 days** might be more common.

For **TechZone**, a **169-day** **CCC** indicates that your cash is tied up for a long time. Ideally, you'd want to shorten that cycle by improving how quickly you move inventory and collect payments from customers.

Vinu: Got it. So, I should aim to reduce my **CCC** by focusing on selling inventory faster and collecting payments quicker. And I can also manage when I pay suppliers to hold onto cash longer.

Manu: Exactly! A shorter **CCC** will give you more cash on hand to reinvest in your business, pay off debts, or cover other expenses. It improves liquidity and helps you run your business more efficiently. Monitoring your **CCC** regularly will help you identify where there are delays and allow you to make adjustments as needed.

Vinu: Thanks, Manu! I'll start tracking my **CCC** closely and work on reducing it by improving inventory turnover and payment collections.

Manu: You're on the right track, Vinu! By optimizing your **Cash Conversion Cycle**, you'll improve your cash flow and have more flexibility to grow **TechZone**. Keep an eye on it, and you'll be able to make smarter financial decisions for your business.

O. Cost of Goods Sold (COGS) Ratio

Manu: Lastly, we have the **COGS Ratio**, which measures the percentage of your sales that goes into producing the goods you sell. This is an important metric because it shows how efficiently you're controlling your **cost of goods sold (COGS)**. A **lower COGS ratio** means you have better cost control in your production or purchasing process, leaving more room for profits.

Vinu: So, the **COGS Ratio** tells me how much of my revenue is being spent on producing my products. If I can lower this ratio, I'll have more left over to cover other expenses and increase profitability, right?

Manu: Exactly! The **COGS Ratio** helps you understand how much of your sales is being used to cover the direct costs of producing your goods. By lowering your **COGS**, you're improving efficiency, which directly translates to higher profitability. Here's the formula:

COGS Ratio = COGS / Revenue

Let's apply this to **TechZone**:

Particulars	₹
COGS	7,00,000
Revenue	12,00,000

COGS - this is the total cost of producing or purchasing the goods you sell, including raw materials, labor, and any other direct costs

Revenue - this is the total sales you generated from selling your gadgets

Now, plugging these into the formula:

COGS Ratio = ₹7,00,000 / ₹12,00,000 = 58.3%

This means that **58.3%** of your revenue is being spent on producing the goods you sell. In other words, for every ₹100 in sales, ₹58.30 goes toward covering the cost of producing your products, leaving ₹41.70 to cover other expenses and generate profit.

Vinu: I see. So, if I reduce my **COGS**, I'll be able to increase my **profit margins** since less of my revenue will be going toward production costs.

Manu: Exactly! Lowering your **COGS** is one of the most effective ways to improve profitability. If you can produce or purchase your goods at a lower cost, you'll have more revenue left over to cover operating expenses like rent, salaries, and marketing—and more profit left over at the end of the day.

Why is the COGS Ratio Important?

1. Measures Cost Efficiency:

The **COGS Ratio** is a direct measure of how efficiently you're managing your production or purchasing costs. A lower ratio means you're able to produce your goods more cost-effectively, which leads to higher profit margins. On the other hand, a high **COGS Ratio** might indicate that your production costs are too high, which can eat into your profits.

2. Impact on Profitability:

Since **COGS** represents the largest expense for most businesses, reducing it has a significant impact on **profit margins**. By keeping your **COGS** under control, you can increase your net profit without necessarily having to increase your sales. Every ₹1 saved in **COGS** goes directly to improving your bottom line.

3. Helps Identify Areas for Improvement:

Monitoring your **COGS Ratio** can help you identify areas where you can improve efficiency, such as negotiating better prices with suppliers, finding cheaper materials, or optimizing your production processes. By continuously working on reducing **COGS**, you can make your business more efficient and profitable over time.

Vinu: So, if I focus on lowering my **COGS**, I can improve **TechZone's** profitability without having to increase sales. That sounds like a great way to boost margins.

Manu: Exactly! The beauty of reducing **COGS** is that it directly improves your **profit margins** without requiring you to sell more. Even small reductions in **COGS** can have a big impact on your bottom line. Let's look at some ways you can reduce your **COGS**.

How Can You Reduce Your COGS?

1. Negotiate Better Supplier Terms:

One of the easiest ways to reduce **COGS** is by negotiating better terms with your suppliers. You can ask for discounts on bulk purchases, explore alternative suppliers, or renegotiate contracts for better pricing. If you can get the same quality materials for a lower price, you'll reduce your overall production costs.

2. Improve Production Efficiency:

Another way to lower **COGS** is by improving your production process. This could involve reducing waste, optimizing labor, or automating certain parts of the process. By making your production line more efficient, you can lower your cost per unit and reduce overall **COGS**.

3. Consider Cheaper Materials:

If possible, consider sourcing cheaper materials that don't compromise on quality. Switching to a more cost-effective material or supplier can significantly reduce your **COGS**. However, it's important to make sure that the quality of your product doesn't suffer, as that could hurt sales in the long run.

4. Reduce Overproduction or Overstocking:

Holding excess inventory can drive up **COGS** if the stock doesn't sell quickly. Consider using **just-in-time (JIT)** inventory management, where you only order or produce stock when you need it. This can help reduce storage costs and avoid tying up cash in unsold inventory.

5. Outsource or Automate Processes:

If there are parts of your production process that are costly, consider outsourcing to third-party providers or automating tasks to reduce labor costs. This can lead to significant savings over time, lowering your **COGS**.

Vinu: Those are great strategies! So, if I can negotiate better supplier prices or make my production more efficient, I'll reduce **COGS** and have more profit left over from each sale.

Manu: Exactly. Lowering your **COGS** improves your **gross profit margins**, which makes your business more profitable overall. Even small improvements in your **COGS Ratio** can lead to a big difference in your bottom line.

What's a Good COGS Ratio?

A "good" **COGS Ratio** depends on the industry:

- In **retail**, a **COGS Ratio** of **50-70%** might be typical, since products are bought in bulk and sold at a markup.

- In **manufacturing**, the **COGS Ratio** might be **60-80%,** depending on the cost of raw materials and labor.

For **TechZone**, a **COGS Ratio of 58.3%** is reasonable, but there's always room to improve. If you can reduce that ratio even by a few percentage points, you'll see a significant increase in your profitability.

Vinu: So, if I can bring my **COGS Ratio** down from **58.3%** to something like **50%**, I'll be able to keep more of my revenue as profit. That sounds like a great way to boost margins.

Manu: Exactly! Lowering your **COGS Ratio** gives you more flexibility with pricing and allows you to generate more profit from every sale. It's one of the best ways to make your business more efficient and sustainable in the long run.

Vinu: Thanks, Manu! I'll definitely focus on reducing my **COGS** by negotiating better terms with suppliers and optimizing my production processes. This seems like a great way to increase **TechZone's** profitability.

Manu: You're on the right track, Vinu! Keep monitoring your **COGS Ratio** and look for ways to improve efficiency. By reducing your **COGS**, you'll be making **TechZone** more profitable, sustainable, and competitive in the market.

Vinu: Wow, there's so much to consider, but these 15 metrics really help me understand what to focus on. By keeping an eye on things like **Gross Profit Margin, Net Profit Margin, DCP, and Cash Conversion Cycle**, I'll have a clear idea of where my business stands and what actions to take.

Manu: Absolutely! Understanding and monitoring these metrics will give you a strong grasp of your business's financial health. Keep tracking them, and you'll be able to make data-driven decisions that can drive TechZone's success.

Chapter 2
Financial Planning and Forecasting

2.1 Budgeting and Forecasting

Vinu: Manu, I've heard a lot about budgeting and forecasting, but I'm not sure why they're so important for entrepreneurs. Can you explain why I need to focus on these?

Manu: Absolutely, Vinu! **Budgeting** and **forecasting** are crucial tools for entrepreneurs because they help you plan for future growth and ensure your business remains sustainable. When you use financial data to create **forecasts** and **budgets**, you can set clear financial goals, allocate resources effectively, and anticipate potential challenges before they arise.

Why Are Budgeting and Forecasting Important for Entrepreneurs?

1. Guides Financial Planning:

Budgeting and forecasting give you a roadmap for the future. By understanding your projected revenue, expenses, and cash flow, you can make informed decisions on how to grow your business. Without these tools, you're essentially running the business blind, which can lead to cash shortages, overspending, or missed growth opportunities.

2. Prepares for Growth and Uncertainty:

Entrepreneurs face constant changes in the market, customer demand, and financial conditions. A well-prepared **budget** and **forecast** allow you to adapt to these changes, whether it's scaling your business during a boom or tightening your finances during tough times. For **TechZone**, this means planning how much inventory to purchase, setting sales targets, and preparing for potential market fluctuations.

3. Enhances Decision-Making:

With a clear **budget** and **forecast**, you'll have better control over spending, revenue expectations, and cash flow. This helps you make decisions based on data rather than guesswork. For example, if **TechZone** is considering expanding into a new market, you can forecast the costs and revenue potential, helping you decide whether it's a smart investment.

The Difference Between Budgeting and Forecasting

Vinu: I see why they're important, but what's the difference between **budgeting** and **forecasting**? Aren't they the same thing?

Manu: Great question! While they're closely related, there are key differences:

- **Budgeting** is about setting a plan for the future. A **budget** outlines how much revenue you expect to generate, how much you plan to spend, and how you'll allocate resources. Think of it as your **financial plan** for a specific period, typically a year. For **TechZone**, a budget would include expected sales, inventory purchases, marketing costs, and employee salaries for the next 12 months.

- **Forecasting**, on the other hand, is about predicting what is likely to happen based on current trends and data. A **forecast** is more flexible and is updated regularly as new data comes in. For **TechZone**, a forecast might predict sales over the next quarter based on recent sales trends, customer demand, and market conditions.

Vinu: So, a **budget** is a fixed plan, while a **forecast** is more about adjusting to real-time changes?

Manu: Exactly! The **budget** sets your financial goals, and the **forecast** helps you adapt as things change. Both are essential for steering your business in the right direction.

On What Basis Should Budgeting and Forecasting Be Prepared?

Vinu: That makes sense. But how do I prepare a budget and a forecast? What should they be based on?

Manu: Good question! Both **budgeting** and **forecasting** should be based on your **historical financial data**, **market trends**, and **business goals**. Let's break it down for **TechZone**:

1. Historical Data:

Start by looking at your past financial performance—sales, expenses, profit margins, and cash flow. This will give you a solid foundation for predicting future trends. For example, if **TechZone** has consistently sold ₹12,00,000 worth of gadgets each year, you can use that data as a base for your forecast.

2. Market Trends:

Consider current market conditions, customer behavior, and any external factors that could impact your business. For **TechZone**, this might mean keeping an eye on tech trends, changes in customer demand for gadgets, or economic shifts that could affect purchasing power.

3. Business Goals:

Your **budget** should align with your long-term business goals. For example, if **TechZone** wants to expand its product line or enter new markets, you'll need to allocate resources in the budget for research, marketing, and inventory.

Vinu: So, I need to use past data and combine that with current market conditions and my future goals to create both my **budget** and **forecast**?

Manu: Exactly! It's about looking at where you've been, where you are now, and where you want to go.

Vinu: Alright, Manu, I get the importance of using past data, market trends, and my goals to create a budget and forecast. But what are the actual steps involved in preparing a budget?

Manu: Great question, Vinu! Let's walk through the steps. Creating a budget involves a systematic approach that helps you align your financial resources with your business goals. Here's how to go about it:

Step 1: Set Clear Financial Goals

Manu: Start by setting specific, measurable financial goals for the budgeting period. These could include revenue targets, profit margins, cost reduction goals, or expansion plans. For instance, if TechZone aims to increase revenue by 20%, you'll need to set targets for each product line or sales channel to contribute to that growth.

Vinu: So, it's about deciding what we want to achieve financially in the upcoming year?

Manu: Exactly! Clear goals give you a target to work toward and guide the rest of the budgeting process.

Step 2: Estimate Revenue

Manu: Next, estimate your expected revenue. Start by looking at historical sales data and considering any upcoming factors that could impact sales, such as seasonal demand, new products, or market changes. If TechZone plans to introduce a new product, factor in the estimated sales from that product line.

Vinu: Do I need to break this down by month or quarter?

Manu: Yes, that's a good idea! Breaking revenue down into monthly or quarterly estimates allows you to adjust as the year progresses. It also helps you spot trends and address any sales dips early on.

Step 3: List Fixed and Variable Costs

Manu: Once you have a revenue estimate, list your fixed and variable costs. Fixed costs are expenses that don't change with production levels, like rent, salaries, and insurance. Variable costs fluctuate with sales volume, such as raw materials and shipping expenses.

Vinu: So, for TechZone, fixed costs would include our office rent and staff salaries, while variable costs might cover things like packaging and delivery for each gadget sold?

Manu: Exactly! Breaking down these costs helps you understand your baseline expenses and where there's room to save.

Step 4: Plan for Capital Expenditures

Manu: Now, think about any capital expenditures (CAPEX) you'll need. These are significant investments in assets like new equipment, software, or expansion to a new location. For TechZone, this could mean purchasing new production machinery or investing in an e-commerce platform.

Vinu: How do I factor these into the budget?

Manu: List these costs separately, as they're one-time expenses that may require special financing or allocation from profits. Make sure they align with your long-term business goals and aren't straining your cash flow.

Step 5: Calculate Expected Cash Flow

Manu: After estimating revenue and expenses, calculate your expected cash flow. This means looking at when cash is likely to come in and go out of your business. For TechZone, if you offer credit terms to customers, factor in the time delay between making a sale and receiving the payment.

Vinu: So, it's not just about having enough revenue, but also ensuring cash flow timing aligns with our expenses?

Manu: Precisely! Cash flow management is essential to keep operations running smoothly. Make sure you're not in a position where you have unpaid bills but not enough cash on hand due to delayed receivables.

Step 6: Allocate Funds to Different Departments

Manu: Allocate funds based on the budget categories that will help you achieve your goals. This could include marketing, R&D, or operations. For example, if TechZone is planning a product launch, allocate a portion of your budget specifically for marketing campaigns and promotional events.

Vinu: How detailed should this allocation be?

Manu: The more detailed, the better. A clear allocation allows each department to plan their activities and prevents overspending. It also makes it easier to track whether you're on target or need to make adjustments.

Step 7: Include a Contingency Fund

Manu: Always set aside a contingency fund for unexpected costs or emergencies. This can cover unforeseen expenses like equipment repairs, sudden increases in raw material prices, or any other surprises that might come up.

Vinu: How much should I allocate for this?

Manu: It depends on your industry, but a good rule of thumb is to set aside about 5-10% of your total budget as a buffer. For TechZone, this fund could help you weather any unanticipated disruptions without impacting day-to-day operations.

Step 8: Review and Adjust

Manu: Once you have a draft budget, review it carefully. Compare it against your historical data to see if it's realistic. Throughout the year, revisit the budget to see if adjustments are necessary, especially if market conditions change or new opportunities arise.

Vinu: So, it's not a "set it and forget it" approach? I'll need to keep an eye on it?

Manu: Exactly, Vinu! Budgeting is an ongoing process. By regularly reviewing and adjusting, you stay aligned with your goals and adapt to changes proactively.

Vinu: Thanks, Manu! This breakdown really clarifies the budgeting process for me. It feels like we're laying down the blueprint for TechZone's financial health.

Sample Budget for TechZone (Yearly)

This budget reflects TechZone's expected revenue, costs, and expenditures over the course of a year. It's based on planned activities and financial targets.

Category	Amount (₹)
Revenue	
Sales	15,00,000
Total Revenue	**15,00,000**
Cost of Goods Sold (COGS)	
Inventory Purchases	5,00,000
Total COGS	**5,00,000**
Gross Profit	**10,00,000**
Operating Expenses	
Marketing	1,00,000
Salaries	3,00,000
Rent	1,20,000
Utilities	60,000
Miscellaneous Expenses	20,000
Total Operating Expenses	**6,00,000**
Operating Profit	**4,00,000**
Other Expenses	
Interest	50,000
Taxes	50,000
Total Other Expenses	**1,00,000**
Net Profit	**3,00,000**

Sample Forecast for TechZone (Quarterly)

This forecast is based on TechZone's trends & expected market conditions over the next quarter. The forecast can be updated monthly or quarterly based on actual data and changes in projections.

Category	Q1 (₹)	Q2 (₹)	Q3 (₹)	Q4 (₹)	Total (₹)
Revenue					
Sales	3,50,000	4,00,000	3,75,000	4,25,000	15,50,000
Total Revenue	**3,50,000**	**4,00,000**	**3,75,000**	**4,25,000**	**15,50,000**
Cost of Goods Sold (COGS)					
Inventory Purchases	1,25,000	1,30,000	1,15,000	1,20,000	4,90,000
Total COGS	**1,25,000**	**1,30,000**	**1,15,000**	**1,20,000**	**4,90,000**
Gross Profit	**2,25,000**	**2,70,000**	**2,60,000**	**3,05,000**	**10,60,000**
Operating Expenses					
Marketing	25,000	30,000	25,000	20,000	1,00,000
Salaries	75,000	75,000	75,000	75,000	3,00,000
Rent	30,000	30,000	30,000	30,000	1,20,000
Utilities	15,000	15,000	15,000	15,000	60,000
Miscellaneous Expenses	5,000	5,000	5,000	5,000	20,000
Total Operating Expenses	**1,50,000**	**1,55,000**	**1,50,000**	**1,45,000**	**6,00,000**
Operating Profit	**75,000**	**1,15,000**	**1,10,000**	**1,60,000**	**4,60,000**
Other Expenses					
Interest	12,500	12,500	12,500	12,500	50,000
Taxes	12,500	12,500	12,500	12,500	50,000
Total Other Expenses	**25,000**	**25,000**	**25,000**	**25,000**	**1,00,000**
Net Profit	**50,000**	**90,000**	**85,000**	**1,35,000**	**3,60,000**

Who Should Handle Budgeting and Forecasting?

Vinu: Who should be responsible for creating the **budget** and **forecast**? Can I do it myself, or do I need outside help?

Manu: It depends on the size and complexity of your business. For a smaller business like **TechZone**, you can certainly handle it yourself, especially if you're comfortable with financial data. However, as your business grows, it may be helpful to involve a **financial advisor, accountant**, or even a **CFO** (Chief Financial Officer). These professionals can bring a level of expertise in creating accurate forecasts and budgets that reflect industry trends and financial best practices.

1. Owner or Entrepreneur:

In the early stages, you as the business owner should be involved in the budgeting and forecasting process. You know your business best and can set realistic financial goals.

2. Accountant or Financial Advisor:

As your business grows, an accountant can help you ensure that your financial data is accurate and provide insights into tax implications, cash flow management, and long-term planning.

3. CFO or Finance Team:

For larger businesses, a **CFO** or a finance team can take over the responsibility of creating detailed budgets and forecasts, allowing you to focus on strategic decisions.

Vinu: So, I can start by handling it myself, but as **TechZone** grows, it's a good idea to bring in professionals who can help me create more detailed and accurate budgets and forecasts.

Manu: Exactly! The more complex your business becomes, the more valuable it is to have experts involved.

How Should You Use Budgeting and Forecasting for Planning and Steering the Organization?

Vinu: Once I have a **budget** and **forecast**, how do I use them to steer **TechZone** in the right direction?

Manu: Your **budget** and **forecast** are key tools for **planning** and **decision-making**. Here's how you can use them:

1. Setting Financial Targets:

Use your **budget** to set clear financial targets for the year. For **TechZone**, this might mean setting a sales target of ₹15,00,000, allocating ₹5,00,000 for inventory, and budgeting ₹1,00,000 for marketing. These targets give you a roadmap for the year.

2. Monitoring Performance:

Compare your actual performance against the **budget** and **forecast** regularly. This allows you to spot discrepancies and adjust your strategy. For example, if **TechZone's** sales are lower than forecasted, you might need to check and if required, invest in more aggressive marketing.

3. Planning for Growth:

Use your **forecast** to plan for growth. If you see that sales are increasing, you can use the forecast to project when you'll need to hire more staff, invest in more inventory, or expand into new markets.

4. Steering the Business:

Your **forecast** should guide day-to-day decisions. If your forecast shows a cash flow shortfall in the next quarter, you can take steps now to improve cash flow, such as reducing expenses or securing short-term financing.

Vinu: So, the **budget** gives me a plan for the year, and the forecast helps me adjust that plan based on what's actually happening?

Manu: Exactly! The **budget** sets the financial goals, and the forecast helps you navigate the changing circumstances.

What Issues Can Be Avoided by Having Budgeting and Forecasting?

Vinu: What kind of issues can I avoid by having a solid **budget** and **forecast** in place?

Manu: There are several issues you can avoid:

1. Cash Flow Problems:

By forecasting your cash flow, you can avoid situations where you run out of cash unexpectedly. For **TechZone**, this means you won't be caught off guard by large expenses like inventory purchases or supplier payments.

2. Overspending:

A **budget** helps you control spending. Without a budget, it's easy to overspend in areas like marketing or hiring. By sticking to a budget, **TechZone** can ensure that every expense is accounted for and aligned with your financial goals.

3. Missed Growth Opportunities:

With a **forecast**, you can spot growth opportunities early. For example, if sales are consistently higher than forecasted, you can plan to expand your product line or enter new markets without stretching your resources too thin.

4. Financial Surprises:

A **forecast** helps you anticipate financial challenges, such as seasonal dips in sales or upcoming large expenses. By forecasting these challenges, **TechZone** can prepare in advance, avoiding financial stress.

5. Inefficient Resource Allocation:

A **budget** ensures that your resources are allocated effectively. Without a budget, you might overspend in one area while under-investing in another. For **TechZone**, this could mean balancing spending between marketing, product development, and operational costs.

Vinu: That's really helpful. It sounds like **budgeting** and **forecasting** are essential for preventing cash flow issues, controlling spending, and spotting growth opportunities early.

Manu: Exactly! By having a solid **budget** and **forecast**, you'll be in a much stronger position to steer **TechZone** toward long-term success, avoid financial pitfalls, and take advantage of growth opportunities.

2.2 Scenario Analysis and Stress Testing

Vinu: Manu, I've heard about Scenario Analysis and Stress Testing in financial planning, but I'm not quite sure how they work. Can you explain how they apply to my business, TechZone?

Manu: Of course, Vinu! Both Scenario Analysis and Stress Testing are great tools for understanding how your business might perform under different future conditions. They help you plan for various situations—good or bad—so you're prepared for risks and opportunities alike.

What is Scenario Analysis?

Manu: Scenario Analysis looks at different potential outcomes based on changes in key factors, like sales or costs. It helps you see how your business would perform under different conditions, such as a best-case, worst-case, or most likely scenario.

Let's apply it to TechZone:

- **Best-case scenario**: Imagine sales grow by 20%, costs stay stable, and demand for your gadgets surges. You'd be in a great position to expand and invest in new products.

- **Worst-case scenario**: Now, picture a drop in sales by 30%, rising production costs, and a component shortage. This would strain your resources, so you'd need to cut expenses and possibly delay projects.

- **Most likely scenario**: Sales grow by 10%, costs increase a bit, and demand remains steady. In this case, you'd continue operations as usual, focusing on gradual growth.

Vinu: So, it's about preparing for different possible outcomes. But how does this help me manage TechZone?

Manu: Exactly! Scenario Analysis helps you anticipate what could happen, so you can make informed decisions no matter what the situation. For example, if you know a sales drop is possible, you might save more cash or cut back on non-essential spending.

What is Stress Testing?

Manu: Stress Testing is a bit different. Instead of looking at various possible scenarios, it focuses on how your business would handle severe, unexpected events. Think of it as testing your business's limits.

For TechZone, Stress Testing might look like this:

- **Major sales drop**: Sales fall by 50% due to a market shift. Could you cover your expenses if that happened?

- **Supply chain issues**: Imagine a sharp increase in costs due to a supply chain crisis. How would you handle the impact on profits?

- **Cash flow crunch**: If customers delayed their payments, could TechZone keep running smoothly?

Vinu: So, it's like pushing my business to the extremes to see if it can survive the worst possible situations?

Manu: Exactly. Stress Testing helps you find out where TechZone is vulnerable. For example, if you see that a sales drop would seriously impact your cash flow, you might consider setting up a line of credit as a backup.

Why Scenario Analysis and Stress Testing Matter

Manu: There are several reasons these tools are important:

- **Prepare for Uncertainty**: You never know what the future holds. By running these tests, you'll be ready for unexpected changes in sales, costs, or the market.

- **Make Better Decisions**: If your Scenario Analysis shows that increasing marketing boosts sales, you might decide to invest more in marketing during a growth phase.

- **Identify Weaknesses**: Stress Testing can show where you're most vulnerable. For example, if TechZone wouldn't survive a significant sales drop, you know you need a financial cushion.

- **Enhance Financial Stability**: By regularly running these tests, you can make sure TechZone stays stable and agile, no matter what comes your way.

Vinu: That makes sense. So it's about being prepared for both the good and the bad, and having plans in place.

Manu: Exactly! These tools let you stay proactive, not just reactive.

Creating Scenarios and Stress Tests for TechZone

Vinu: How do I go about creating these scenarios and stress tests? What should I base them on?

Manu: Start with these three areas:

- **Historical Data**: Look at how TechZone performed in the past. If you experienced a 10% sales dip during a previous downturn, use that to create a worst-case scenario.

- **Market Trends**: Consider current market conditions. For example, are there new competitors or changes in customer preferences? Factor these into your scenarios.

- **Potential Risks and Opportunities**: Think about what could go right or wrong. What if a key supplier raises prices or if a new opportunity arises to expand into a growing market?

Vinu: So, I'm looking at past performance, market trends, and any possible risks or opportunities?

Manu: Exactly! Use these elements to build realistic scenarios for both good and bad conditions.

Who Should Conduct Scenario Analysis and Stress Testing?

Vinu: Who should handle these analyses? Should I do them myself, or should I bring in outside help?

Manu: Initially, you can handle them yourself, especially if you're comfortable with TechZone's financial data. As the business grows, you might consider hiring professionals to make these analyses more accurate:

- **Business Owner**: You know TechZone best, so you can start by creating basic scenarios and stress tests.

- **Financial Advisor or Analyst**: If TechZone becomes more complex, a financial advisor or analyst can help refine your scenarios and align them with industry trends.

- **CFO or Finance Team**: For larger businesses, a CFO or finance team can conduct regular Scenario Analysis and Stress Testing as part of strategic planning.

Vinu: So, I can start by doing it myself and bring in experts as TechZone grows?

Manu: Exactly. Experts can help you create detailed scenarios and ensure you're fully prepared for any risks.

Using Scenario Analysis and Stress Testing for Business Planning

Vinu: Once I've created these scenarios and stress tests, how do I use them to steer TechZone in the right direction?

Manu: You can use them to guide your planning and strategy:

- **Identify Risks**: By running different scenarios, you can pinpoint potential risks, like a cash shortage, and plan to secure funding if necessary.

- **Adjust Your Strategy**: If a best-case scenario shows potential for growth, consider expanding or increasing marketing efforts. For worst-case scenarios, you might plan to cut non-essential expenses.

- **Create Contingency Plans**: Stress Testing helps you prepare for extreme situations, like a sales drop or cost spike. You can set up contingency plans, such as securing a line of credit, to manage through tough times.

- **Regular Updates**: Revisit your scenarios and stress tests as new data becomes available, so you're always prepared to make strategic adjustments.

Vinu: So, I can use these analyses to identify risks, adjust strategies, and make sure I'm prepared for unexpected challenges?

Manu: Exactly! By regularly conducting Scenario Analysis and Stress Testing, you're putting TechZone in a strong position to handle uncertainties and grow effectively.

Issues That Scenario Analysis and Stress Testing Can Prevent

Vinu: What kind of problems can I avoid by doing this type of analysis?

Manu: You can avoid several key issues:

- **Financial Surprises**: You'll be ready for unexpected events, like a supplier price hike, and can adjust before it impacts your business.

- **Cash Flow Problems**: By spotting potential cash shortages, you can secure financing or adjust expenses ahead of time.

- **Missed Growth Opportunities**: Best-case scenarios show growth opportunities, allowing you to capitalize on strong demand.

- **Business Disruptions**: Stress Testing prepares you for extreme situations, like a supply chain disruption. You'll have plans in place to keep TechZone running smoothly, even under pressure.

Vinu: That sounds really helpful. I'll start running these tests for TechZone to be ready for both the ups and downs.

Manu: That's the right approach, Vinu! With Scenario Analysis and Stress Testing, you'll be prepared for growth opportunities and resilient enough to handle challenges.

Chapter 3 - Cash Flow and Working Capital Management

3.1 Mastering Inventory Management for Better Profit Margins

Vinu: Manu, I've been noticing that sometimes we have too much inventory, and other times, we run out of popular products. It feels like I'm always trying to catch up. How can I manage TechZone's inventory better to improve profits and reduce losses?

Manu: That's a great question, Vinu! Inventory management is crucial for maintaining healthy cash flow and improving profit margins. Effective inventory management means having the right amount of stock on hand—enough to meet customer demand but not so much that it ties up your cash unnecessarily. Let's look at some key areas you should focus on to make inventory work for TechZone.

1. Forecasting Demand Accurately

Vinu: I've tried to predict demand based on past sales, but sometimes I still end up with excess stock or shortages. How can I improve my forecasting?

Manu: Accurate demand forecasting is essential. Start by analyzing past sales data to identify trends and seasonality. For example, if TechZone typically sells more gadgets around the holiday season, you'll want to increase inventory ahead of that peak. However, if you notice slower sales during certain months, you can reduce stock accordingly.

Use tools like sales reports and inventory management software that tracks sales patterns. Also, consider external factors, like market trends and economic conditions. These factors can influence customer demand, helping you make more accurate predictions.

Vinu: So, it's about combining past data with current market trends to get a clearer picture of future demand?

Manu: Exactly! By using historical data and staying informed about trends, you can better anticipate when demand will spike or slow down, and plan your inventory accordingly.

2. Implementing Just-in-Time (JIT) Inventory

Vinu: I've heard of Just-in-Time inventory, but I'm not sure how it works. Can it help TechZone?

Manu: Just-in-Time (JIT) inventory is a method where you order and receive stock just as you need it for sales or production. This reduces the amount of inventory you need to keep on hand, which in turn frees up cash and reduces storage costs.

For example, if TechZone knows it needs 100 units of a particular gadget each month, you can arrange to receive these units weekly instead of all at once. This way, you're not sitting on excess stock, and you can adjust orders based on demand. However, JIT requires good relationships with reliable suppliers who can deliver on short notice.

Vinu: That sounds helpful, especially for reducing the costs of holding too much inventory. Are there any risks with JIT?

Manu: Yes, JIT can save costs, but it also has risks. If there's a supply chain disruption, you might face stockouts and delays. That's why it's important to have backup suppliers or a small safety stock for high-demand items. JIT works best when you have predictable demand and reliable suppliers.

3. Managing Stock Levels with ABC Analysis

Vinu: What's the best way to prioritize inventory items? TechZone has a mix of high-value gadgets and low-cost accessories, and I feel like they need different levels of attention.

Manu: You're absolutely right. Not all inventory items require the same level of attention. This is where **ABC Analysis** can help. In ABC Analysis, you categorize inventory into three groups:

- **A Items**: These are high-value items with lower sales frequency. They need careful monitoring because they have a big impact on profitability. For TechZone, this might be your premium gadgets that are more expensive but sell less frequently.

- **B Items**: These are mid-value items that have a moderate impact on your inventory cost. They need less frequent monitoring than A items but still require regular attention. For example, mid-range gadgets that sell consistently but don't generate as much revenue as A items.

- **C Items**: These are low-value items with high sales frequency. They don't impact your bottom line as much individually but are important for customer satisfaction. Accessories like chargers or cases could fall into this category for TechZone.

By focusing on A items more closely, you ensure you're managing your most valuable stock carefully. B and C items can be managed with simpler controls.

Vinu: That makes sense! So, the A items need tight controls, and I can manage the B and C items with a lighter touch?

Manu: Exactly. By segmenting your inventory, you can allocate resources and attention more effectively, improving your overall profitability and reducing the risk of excess stock or shortages.

4. Reducing Inventory Costs by Managing Storage Efficiently

Vinu: We spend quite a bit on storage. Is there a way to cut down on these costs?

Manu: Storage costs can add up quickly, especially if you're holding onto excess stock. One way to reduce these costs is by **optimizing your storage layout**. Make sure high-demand items are easily accessible to reduce time and handling costs. For TechZone, you might place frequently sold gadgets near the front to streamline picking and packing.

Another approach is **outsourcing storage** to a third-party logistics provider. They can manage the storage and shipping for you, reducing your storage overhead and freeing up space. Alternatively, if you own the storage space, you could lease out any excess storage space to other businesses.

Vinu: Those are great ideas. Are there any other ways to manage inventory costs?

Manu: Absolutely. You can also focus on **reducing dead stock**—products that aren't selling. Dead stock takes up valuable storage space and ties up cash. Identify these items through inventory reports, then consider discounting or bundling them to move them out faster. This clears space for higher-demand products and improves cash flow.

5. Using Inventory Turnover Ratio for Better Decision-Making

Vinu: How do I know if my inventory management practices are working well?

Manu: A great metric to track is your **Inventory Turnover Ratio**. This ratio shows how many times you sell and replace your inventory over a specific period. A high turnover ratio means you're selling products quickly and not holding onto excess stock, which is ideal. A low turnover ratio suggests you have too much stock or that sales are slow.

To calculate it, divide the **Cost of Goods Sold (COGS)** by the **average inventory**. For example, if TechZone's COGS is ₹10,00,000 and the average inventory is ₹2,00,000, then your Inventory Turnover Ratio is 5. This means you're turning over inventory five times a year.

Vinu: So, a higher turnover ratio is better because it indicates efficient inventory management?

Manu: Yes, a higher ratio is generally better, but it depends on your industry and product type. Compare your ratio to industry standards to see if you're on track. Monitoring this ratio regularly helps you make adjustments and ensures your inventory management strategy aligns with business goals.

6. Avoiding Common Inventory Management Mistakes

Vinu: What are some common mistakes I should avoid with inventory management?

Manu: Here are a few key mistakes to watch out for:

- **Over-ordering**: Buying too much stock ties up cash and increases storage costs. Stick to your demand forecasts and don't let promotions or supplier discounts tempt you into overstocking.

- **Not tracking stock regularly**: Infrequent inventory checks can lead to unnoticed losses, like theft or damage. Regular audits keep you informed about your stock levels and reduce errors.

- **Neglecting reorder points**: Failing to set reorder points can lead to stockouts. For high-demand items, establish reorder points so you know when to place a new order before you run out.

- **Ignoring slow-moving items**: As we discussed, dead stock takes up space and ties up cash. Regularly review slow-moving items and have a plan to clear them out.

- **Failing to use technology**: Relying on manual tracking can lead to errors. Inventory management software provides accurate, real-time data, helping you make informed decisions.

Vinu: Those are really helpful tips. I can see how over-ordering and not using technology could create problems.

Manu: Exactly. Good inventory management reduces waste, keeps costs down, and improves profitability. Using software and setting up a regular review process helps you stay on top of inventory levels and respond quickly to changes in demand.

Vinu: Thanks, Manu. This has been eye-opening. I feel like I have a much better handle on how to manage TechZone's inventory effectively and avoid the common mistakes.

Manu: You're welcome, Vinu! Remember, inventory management isn't just about keeping stock on hand—it's about optimizing resources to boost profitability and ensure customer satisfaction. Now that you've got a strong foundation in inventory management, you're well on your way to running a leaner, more efficient business.

3.2 Mastering Receivables Management for Better Cash Flow

Vinu: Manu, I've been noticing that some of our customers take a long time to pay. I feel like it's affecting TechZone's cash flow. What can I do to manage receivables better and make sure we're getting paid on time?

Manu: Great question, Vinu! Managing receivables is crucial for maintaining healthy cash flow. When customers delay payments, it ties up your cash and can even hurt profitability. Let's look at some key areas you can focus on to improve receivables management and keep TechZone's cash flow strong.

1. Setting Clear Payment Terms

Vinu: I usually let customers pay within 30 days, but some still take longer. What can I do to make sure they stick to the terms?

Manu: Setting clear payment terms from the beginning is essential. Make sure your payment terms are straightforward and agreed upon before any sale. For example, instead of saying "Net 30 days," you could specify, "Payment is due within 30 days of the invoice date."

Another helpful tip is to add an incentive for early payments. For instance, offer a 2% discount if customers pay within 10 days. This encourages them to pay faster, which improves cash flow.

Vinu: So, making the terms clear and offering a small discount can motivate customers to pay on time?

Manu: Exactly! And when terms are clear, there's less room for confusion. It's a small step that can make a big difference in how quickly you get paid.

2. Conducting Credit Checks for New Customers

Vinu: We're always looking for new customers, but I worry about whether they'll pay on time. Is there a way to assess a new customer's creditworthiness before doing business with them?

Manu: Yes, you can conduct a **credit check** before extending credit to new customers. This will give you insight into their payment history and whether they have a record of late payments or unpaid debts. For TechZone, if you're considering a big order for a new client, you can ask for references or use a credit agency to check their financial standing.

If a customer has a poor credit history, you might require a partial upfront payment or stick to a shorter payment term, like Net 15 instead of Net 30. This reduces your risk if they end up paying late.

Vinu: That sounds smart. So, if we're dealing with a new customer, we should assess their credit first to minimize potential risks?

Manu: Exactly. Not every customer is the right fit for credit terms. By conducting credit checks, you're protecting TechZone from potential cash flow issues caused by late or missed payments.

3. Invoicing Promptly and Accurately

Vinu: Sometimes we take a while to send invoices, especially during busy periods. How does this affect our receivables?

Manu: Delays in invoicing lead to delays in payment. The sooner you send an invoice, the sooner the payment clock starts ticking. Aim to send invoices immediately after delivering the product or service. You can even automate the process with accounting software, which generates and sends invoices as soon as an order is fulfilled.

Also, make sure invoices are accurate. Errors, like incorrect amounts or missing details, can lead to payment delays as the customer may need clarification. For TechZone, having a standardized invoicing template can ensure you always include the necessary details—like the due date, payment terms, and any discounts offered for early payment.

Vinu: So, being prompt and accurate with invoices can help speed up payments and reduce any back-and-forth?

Manu: Absolutely. Timely and accurate invoicing sends a message that you take payments seriously and want to avoid any unnecessary delays. Plus, it helps customers prioritize your invoices over others.

4. Establishing a Follow-Up System for Overdue Payments

Vinu: Sometimes I feel awkward following up on overdue payments. What's the best way to do it without straining customer relationships?

Manu: It's normal to feel that way, but a friendly follow-up is part of doing business. Start with a gentle reminder a few days before the due date. After that, set a schedule for follow-ups—perhaps 7, 14, and 30 days past due.

For example, TechZone could send an email reminder on day 7, followed by a phone call on day 14 if the payment hasn't arrived. Keep the tone friendly and professional. Sometimes customers genuinely forget, and a polite nudge is all they need.

Vinu: What if a customer still doesn't pay after multiple reminders?

Manu: If a customer consistently ignores reminders, it's time to consider additional steps. For larger amounts, you could consider a collection agency, but this should be a last resort. In some cases, you may also want to stop providing credit terms to that customer until they catch up on payments.

Remember, you're running a business, and it's fair to expect timely payments. If a customer can't commit, it may be best to reassess their terms.

5. Offering Multiple Payment Options

Vinu: I've noticed that some customers request different payment methods. Would offering more options actually speed up payments?

Manu: Yes, giving customers convenient payment options can make it easier for them to pay on time. Consider offering options like bank transfers, credit cards, or digital wallets. For TechZone, you could also enable online payment links in your invoices, allowing customers to pay immediately.

Vinu: That's a good idea. So, by offering more options, we're accommodating customers' preferences and potentially reducing the wait time for payments?

Manu: Exactly. Some customers may prefer to pay via credit card or digital wallet, and by offering these options, you remove barriers to payment. This flexibility can encourage prompt payments and reduce outstanding receivables.

6. Monitoring Accounts Receivable Aging

Vinu: How do I know if my receivables management strategy is working?

Manu: A great way to measure this is by using an **Accounts Receivable Aging Report**. This report categorizes outstanding invoices by how long they've been overdue—30, 60, 90 days, and so on. Ideally, most of your receivables should be within the current or 30-day period.

For TechZone, if you see many invoices in the 60- or 90-day categories, it indicates a potential cash flow problem. Regularly reviewing the aging report lets you spot overdue accounts quickly and focus on collecting those payments.

Vinu: So, if I notice too many overdue payments, I need to follow up more frequently and maybe rethink some customer terms?

Manu: Exactly. The aging report helps you stay proactive. If you see trends—like certain customers always paying late—you can make adjustments, such as shorter terms or requiring partial upfront payments.

7. Avoiding Common Mistakes in Receivables Management

Vinu: Are there any common mistakes I should watch out for with receivables management?

Manu: Definitely! Here are a few to avoid:

- **Extending Credit Too Freely**: Not every customer should get credit terms. If you're too lenient, you may end up with a large amount of unpaid receivables. Always assess creditworthiness first.

- **Not Following Up on Overdue Accounts**: Waiting too long to follow up sends the message that you don't take payment terms seriously. It's important to have a consistent follow-up process.

- **Ignoring Payment History**: If you keep providing credit to customers who consistently pay late, it can harm cash flow. Reassess terms for customers with poor payment histories.

- **Failing to Monitor Cash Flow**: If you're not tracking receivables, it's easy to overlook delayed payments and only realize there's a problem when cash runs low.

- **Not Automating Invoicing**: Manual invoicing can lead to delays and errors. Automation speeds up the process and reduces mistakes, helping you get paid faster.

Vinu: I see how these mistakes could lead to cash flow problems. I'll make sure we avoid them at TechZone.

Manu: Great plan, Vinu. Effective receivables management isn't just about collecting money—it's about keeping cash flowing so TechZone can grow. By setting clear terms, offering flexible payment options, and following up consistently, you're ensuring the business stays on strong financial footing.

Vinu: Thanks, Manu. I feel much more confident about managing receivables now. It seems like small changes, like setting clearer terms and following up, can make a big difference.

Manu: Absolutely! Receivables management is key to maintaining healthy cash flow and preventing losses. Now that you have a solid foundation, let's move on to **payables management** in the next chapter. Knowing how to manage both receivables and payables keeps the business financially balanced.

Vinu: I'm ready for it. Let's dive into managing payables!

3.3 Effective Payables Management for Better Financial Control

Vinu: Manu, we've talked about managing receivables, but I also want to make sure we're handling our payables correctly. Are there specific strategies for managing what TechZone owes to suppliers and vendors?

Manu: Absolutely, Vinu! Just as managing receivables ensures that you're getting paid on time, managing payables effectively helps you control cash flow, reduce costs, and build strong relationships with suppliers. Good payables management is all about making the most of your payment terms and ensuring you're using resources wisely. Let's look at some areas where you can improve payables management for TechZone.

1. Taking Advantage of Payment Terms

Vinu: Sometimes we pay our suppliers as soon as we get the invoice, just to get it off our plate. Is there a benefit to waiting until the due date?

Manu: Yes, Vinu. Paying early isn't always necessary, and by doing so, you could miss out on opportunities to keep cash in the business longer. If you have payment terms of, say, Net 30 days, take full advantage of that time. By holding onto the cash until closer to the due date, you improve cash flow and have more funds available for other expenses or investments.

However, if a supplier offers a discount for early payment, like 2% if paid within 10 days, it's worth considering. For TechZone, saving 2% on a ₹1,00,000 purchase would be ₹2,000. That's a nice saving if your cash flow allows you to take advantage of it.

Vinu: So, if there's no early payment discount, I should wait until the due date to pay? That way, I can keep cash on hand longer.

Manu: Exactly. Think of payment terms as an interest-free loan. It's best to utilize that time for other needs if you're not receiving an early payment incentive.

2. Building Strong Relationships with Suppliers

Vinu: We usually don't interact much with suppliers beyond placing orders and paying invoices. Is there value in building stronger relationships with them?

Manu: Definitely! Strong supplier relationships can lead to better terms, priority during busy times, and flexibility in payment arrangements. For example, if TechZone has a good relationship with a supplier, they might extend payment terms during a cash crunch, or offer bulk discounts on larger orders. Building rapport can create mutual trust and open the door to these kinds of arrangements.

Take the time to meet with your key suppliers, discuss your business goals, and see how you can work together. Good communication also ensures that if any issues arise, like delayed shipments, you can resolve them quickly.

Vinu: So, connecting with suppliers beyond the transaction level can help us get better terms and build flexibility into our payables?

Manu: Exactly. Suppliers are more likely to offer favorable terms to businesses they trust. And for TechZone, that can mean cost savings and improved cash flow management.

3. Prioritizing Payables Strategically

Vinu: We have several vendors we pay each month. How do I know which invoices to prioritize if we're tight on cash?

Manu: That's a smart question. If cash flow is tight, prioritize invoices based on a few key factors:

- **Essential Suppliers**: Pay suppliers who are critical to your operations first. For TechZone, this might be your primary gadget suppliers. Without them, you can't meet customer demand.

- **Early Payment Discounts**: If a supplier offers an early payment discount, consider paying them sooner to capture that savings.

- **Late Payment Penalties**: Some vendors charge late fees. Pay those on time to avoid unnecessary costs.

- **Interest Rates**: If you're carrying any debt, compare the cost of paying that down against potential late fees on invoices. This helps you prioritize the highest cost obligations first.

By using this approach, you ensure that TechZone keeps essential operations running smoothly and avoids unnecessary costs.

Vinu: So, if we're ever in a cash crunch, I should focus on key suppliers, discounts, and fees. That way, we're making the most financially sound decisions?

Manu: Exactly, Vinu. Prioritizing strategically helps you avoid disruptions and manage cash flow during tight periods.

4. Avoiding Common Payables Management Mistakes

Vinu: Are there any common mistakes to watch out for when managing payables?

Manu: Definitely! Here are a few common mistakes that can affect cash flow and supplier relationships:

- **Paying Too Early Without a Discount**: Like we discussed, paying invoices right away without any incentive ties up cash unnecessarily. Always take advantage of payment terms.

- **Missing Payment Due Dates**: Late payments can hurt relationships and lead to late fees. Set up reminders or use accounting software to ensure timely payments.

- **Overlooking Invoice Errors**: Mistakes on invoices happen, and if you're not checking them, you might pay more than you owe. Always review invoices for accuracy.

- **Failing to Negotiate Terms**: Suppliers may offer better terms, especially if you're a long-term customer. Don't be afraid to negotiate payment terms that suit TechZone's cash flow better.

- **Relying Too Much on One Supplier**: If you only rely on one supplier, you risk disruptions if they face issues. Diversify suppliers where possible to reduce risk.

Vinu: I hadn't thought about checking invoices closely or negotiating terms. It seems like these small details can really impact cash flow.

Manu: Exactly! Attention to detail and negotiating terms can have a significant effect on your cash flow and overall financial health. By avoiding these common mistakes, you ensure better control over payables and maintain good relationships with suppliers.

5. Using Technology to Manage Payables Efficiently

Vinu: We've been handling payables manually, but I've heard that software can make the process easier. How can technology help with managing payables?

Manu: Great question, Vinu. Using accounting or payables management software can automate and streamline the process. Here's how it can help:

- **Automated Reminders**: Software can send you reminders for upcoming payments, so you never miss a due date. For TechZone, this means avoiding late fees and protecting your supplier relationships.

- **Invoice Tracking**: With software, you can track invoices in real time, see which are due soon, and prioritize payments. You can also keep digital copies, reducing paperwork and making it easier to find records if there's a dispute.

- **Payment Scheduling**: You can schedule payments for future dates, aligning them with your cash flow. This way, you're paying on the due date without having to remember each deadline manually.

- **Better Cash Flow Forecasting**: Many tools offer cash flow forecasting, so you can plan your payables around projected cash inflows. This gives you a clearer view of your financial position and helps you make informed decisions.

Vinu: That sounds really helpful. Using technology would save time and make sure we're staying on top of payments more efficiently.

Manu: Exactly. By automating these tasks, you reduce the risk of human error, improve cash flow management, and free up time to focus on growing TechZone.

6. Monitoring Key Payables Metrics

Vinu: Are there any specific metrics I should be tracking to know if our payables management is on track?

Manu: Yes, keeping an eye on a few key metrics can provide insights into the health of your payables management. Here are a couple of important ones:

- **Days Payable Outstanding (DPO)**: This metric shows the average number of days TechZone takes to pay its suppliers. A higher DPO means you're taking full advantage of payment terms, but if it's too high, it could strain supplier relationships.

- **Accounts Payable Turnover Ratio**: This ratio indicates how quickly you're paying off suppliers. A higher ratio means you're paying off debts quickly, while a lower ratio suggests you're holding onto cash longer.

- **Cash Conversion Cycle (CCC)**: The CCC measures the time it takes for cash to flow back into the business. It's the combination of receivables, inventory, and payables. Monitoring this cycle helps you understand the overall cash flow efficiency.

Tracking these metrics regularly can help you make better decisions about when to pay suppliers and manage cash flow effectively.

Vinu: So, by watching these metrics, I can get a clearer picture of how well we're managing payables and make adjustments as needed?

Manu: Exactly! Monitoring DPO, the payables turnover ratio, and the CCC gives you valuable insights into cash flow. It helps you balance between timely payments and holding cash as long as possible.

Vinu: Thanks, Manu. This makes a lot more sense now. I can see how managing payables strategically can improve TechZone's cash flow and even strengthen our supplier relationships.

Manu: You're welcome, Vinu! Good payables management is all about timing and making smart choices with your resources. When you're proactive, you not only improve cash flow but also create opportunities for discounts and better terms with suppliers.

3.4 Mastering Cash & Bank Balances Management for better Liquidity

Vinu: Manu, Are there specific strategies for managing cash and bank balances better?

Manu: Absolutely, Vinu! Cash management is all about making sure that TechZone has the right amount of cash on hand for day-to-day needs while also putting surplus cash to work. It's essential for maximizing profitability and reducing losses. Let's go over some areas that can make a big difference in how you manage cash.

1. Maintaining an Optimal Cash Balance

Vinu: I often wonder how much cash we should keep on hand. Should we be aiming for a specific amount?

Manu: Great question. It's important to maintain an **optimal cash balance**. You don't want to hold too much cash, as that's money that could be invested or used for growth. But you also need enough on hand to cover operational expenses and handle unexpected costs.

For TechZone, start by calculating your average monthly expenses and keep a reserve for at least three months of operating costs. This gives you a safety net while avoiding an excess cash balance that isn't being used productively.

Vinu: So, having enough to cover three months of expenses is a good benchmark?

Manu: Yes, that's a good rule of thumb. By maintaining a reserve, you ensure that you're prepared for any unexpected expenses or slow periods without holding too much idle cash.

2. Regularly Reconciling Bank Statements

Vinu: I haven't been as consistent as I should be with reconciling our bank statements. How important is it?

Manu: Regular **bank reconciliation** is essential. It ensures that your cash records match the actual bank balances and helps you catch errors, such as unauthorized transactions, bank fees, or even missed payments.

For TechZone, reconcile your bank statements at least once a month. This process gives you an accurate picture of your cash position and helps you catch discrepancies early, which can reduce losses due to errors or fraud.

Vinu: I see. By reconciling regularly, we're not only keeping accurate records but also identifying any potential issues right away.

Manu: Exactly. Bank reconciliation is a simple practice, but it has a big impact on your cash management and accuracy of your financial records.

3. Accelerating Collections and Delaying Payments

Vinu: How can we manage the timing of cash inflows and outflows to improve cash management?

Manu: Great question, Vinu. One way to improve cash management is by **accelerating collections** from customers while **delaying payments** to suppliers, within the terms agreed upon, of course.

For instance, if TechZone can offer a small discount to customers who pay within 10 days, you're likely to see cash coming in faster. On the flip side, if your suppliers offer 30-day terms, use the full period to keep cash in the business longer. By optimizing these timings, you maximize the cash on hand without any additional cost.

Vinu: So it's about being strategic with when cash comes in and goes out. This way, we have more control over our cash balances?

Manu: Exactly. It's a balancing act. By aligning collections and payments strategically, you create a smoother cash flow and reduce the need for additional financing.

4. Investing Surplus Cash Wisely

Vinu: We sometimes end up with surplus cash. Should we just leave it in our bank account, or is there a better way to use it?

Manu: Leaving surplus cash in a regular bank account might not be the most productive choice. Look for **short-term investment options** that offer better returns while still providing liquidity.

For example, TechZone could consider options like a high-yield savings account, short-term fixed deposits, or a money market account. These can earn you interest, which helps improve profitability. Just make sure the investment is liquid, meaning you can access the cash quickly if needed.

Vinu: That makes sense. So by putting surplus cash into short-term investments, we can earn a bit extra without risking our liquidity?

Manu: Exactly! It's about finding a balance between keeping cash accessible and maximizing returns on idle funds.

5. Controlling Cash Leakage

Vinu: I've heard that cash leakage can impact profitability, but what does it mean exactly?

Manu: Cash leakage refers to small expenses or inefficiencies that drain cash over time. These are often overlooked but can add up and impact your bottom line. For example, unplanned purchases, unnecessary bank fees, or even employee expenses that aren't tracked closely can lead to cash leakage.

For TechZone, track all expenses and keep an eye on recurring charges. Are there subscriptions or fees you're paying for that aren't adding value? Reducing these unnecessary expenses can improve your profit margin.

Vinu: So it's about eliminating wasteful expenses and making sure we're only spending on what truly benefits the business?

Manu: Exactly. Small, unnecessary expenses may seem minor, but over time, they reduce profits. Controlling cash leakage helps keep more cash in the business and improves overall profitability.

6. Managing Cash Flow Seasonality

Vinu: Our sales tend to fluctuate seasonally. How can I manage cash flow during both peak and slow periods?

Manu: If TechZone has seasonal highs and lows, you'll need a plan to **manage cash flow seasonality**. During peak seasons, make an effort to build up your cash reserves. This way, you'll have funds to cover expenses during slower months.

Consider using short-term financing options, like a line of credit, to cover expenses if needed during slow periods. But be cautious—only borrow what you're confident you can repay once sales pick up again.

Vinu: So, if we build reserves during busy times, we'll be in a better position to handle slower periods without relying too much on credit?

Manu: Exactly. Planning for seasonality helps you avoid cash shortages and keeps TechZone running smoothly all year round.

7. Implementing Cash Flow Forecasting

Vinu: We've done some cash flow forecasting, but I'm not sure how often we should be doing it. How frequently should we update these forecasts?

Manu: Ideally, you should **update your cash flow forecasts** monthly. This helps you anticipate any cash shortfalls or surpluses and make adjustments accordingly. A forecast allows you to plan for upcoming expenses, identify when you'll need extra cash, and avoid surprises.

For TechZone, updating your forecast regularly means you're prepared for slow months and can make informed decisions about investments or spending. With regular forecasting, you gain control over your cash position and can make proactive decisions.

Vinu: Got it. Regular forecasting gives us a roadmap for cash management, so we're always a step ahead?

Manu: Exactly. It's all about staying proactive. By forecasting regularly, you have a clear picture of your cash needs and can plan accordingly.

8. Monitoring Key Cash Management Metrics

Vinu: Are there specific metrics I should track to see how well we're managing cash?

Manu: Yes, monitoring certain metrics gives you insight into how effectively you're managing cash. Here are a few to consider:

- **Cash Conversion Cycle (CCC):** This measures how long it takes to convert investments in inventory and other resources into cash. A shorter CCC is better, as it means you're converting resources to cash more quickly.

- **Current Ratio:** This ratio compares your current assets to current liabilities, helping you understand if you have enough liquidity to cover short-term obligations.

- **Cash Flow from Operations:** This shows how much cash your business generates from its core activities. A positive cash flow indicates you're covering expenses and generating surplus cash.

Tracking these metrics regularly helps you gauge the health of your cash management strategy and spot areas for improvement.

Vinu: So by monitoring these metrics, I can get a clearer picture of where TechZone stands financially and make better cash management decisions?

Manu: Absolutely. These metrics give you a snapshot of your financial health and help you make informed decisions to keep cash flow steady.

Vinu: Thanks, Manu. This really helps me understand how effective cash management can improve profitability and reduce losses. I'll definitely start tracking these areas more closely.

Manu: You're welcome, Vinu! Cash management is key to a healthy, sustainable business. When you control your cash well, you not only support daily operations but also create opportunities for growth.

3.5 Mastering Expense Management for Higher Profit Margins

Vinu: Manu, we've covered cash flow and cash management, but I feel like our expenses are all over the place. How can we get better control over what we're spending to improve TechZone's profit margins?

Manu: Great question, Vinu! Managing expenses effectively is crucial for maximizing profits. By keeping an eye on different types of expenses—like direct, indirect, selling, and administrative costs—you can make better decisions about where to save, invest, or cut back. Let's break it down and go over strategies for each type of expense to help TechZone stay profitable.

1. Direct Expenses

Vinu: Let's start with direct expenses. These seem pretty straightforward—aren't they just the costs of making or buying our products?

Manu: Yes, exactly! **Direct expenses** are directly tied to the production of goods or services. For TechZone, this includes costs like raw materials, manufacturing costs, and any labor specifically tied to producing your gadgets.

To manage direct expenses effectively:

- **Negotiate with Suppliers**: Regularly review and renegotiate prices with your suppliers. If TechZone buys materials in larger quantities, you might be able to get bulk discounts, which reduces per-unit costs.

- **Reduce Waste**: Look at ways to optimize production processes. For example, if there's a lot of material waste, consider changing suppliers, redesigning products, or training employees on efficient usage.

- **Outsource When Feasible**: In some cases, outsourcing specific production tasks can reduce costs. If TechZone has certain components that can be made cheaper elsewhere, it might be worth exploring that option.

Vinu: So, for direct expenses, it's about negotiating, reducing waste, and finding cost-effective solutions. I can see how even small savings here would add up.

Manu: Exactly, Vinu! Since direct expenses directly impact your cost of goods sold, controlling them can significantly improve profit margins.

2. Indirect Expenses

Vinu: What about indirect expenses? They seem a bit more challenging to control.

Manu: Indirect expenses are indeed a bit trickier since they support overall business operations but aren't tied directly to production. For TechZone, **indirect expenses** might include utilities, rent, and equipment maintenance.

To manage indirect expenses:

- **Monitor Utility Usage**: Encourage energy-saving practices, such as turning off equipment when not in use or using energy-efficient lighting. This helps reduce utility bills.

- **Negotiate Rent and Maintenance Contracts**: Don't be afraid to negotiate lease terms or maintenance contracts. For example, if your lease is up for renewal, see if you can get better terms based on your long-term occupancy.

- **Review Regularly**: Set aside time to review these expenses periodically. You may find opportunities to cut costs, like switching to a more affordable internet provider or reducing unnecessary maintenance services.

Vinu: So indirect expenses are more about optimizing ongoing costs, like utilities and rent, to keep things running efficiently?

Manu: Exactly. Reducing indirect expenses may not seem like a big deal on its own, but combined savings on these items can significantly improve your overall profitability.

3. Selling Expenses

Vinu: I get that we have to spend money to market and sell our products, but I sometimes wonder if we're spending in the right areas. How can we manage our selling expenses better?

Manu: Great question, Vinu. **Selling expenses** include all costs related to marketing, advertising, and sales efforts. For TechZone, this might cover things like online ads, promotional materials, or even salaries for sales staff.

Here's how to manage these costs:

- **Analyze Marketing ROI**: For each marketing channel, calculate the return on investment (ROI). If certain ads are bringing in more sales, focus on those, and reduce spending on channels with lower returns. For instance, if social media ads yield more customers than print ads, adjust your budget accordingly.

- **Use Low-Cost Marketing Options**: Leverage digital marketing tactics like social media, email marketing, and content marketing. These tend to be more cost-effective than traditional methods and offer good reach.

- **Train Your Sales Team**: Equip your sales team with skills that help close sales faster. Efficient sales processes mean your team spends less time and money on each sale. Training them on negotiation and objection handling, for example, can improve conversion rates and reduce per-customer acquisition costs.

Vinu: So by measuring our marketing spend and focusing on what works, we can get better results without increasing our budget?

Manu: Exactly! It's all about smart spending. By channeling funds into marketing methods that generate the highest ROI, TechZone can maximize impact while controlling costs.

4. General & Administrative (G&A) Expenses

Vinu: How about general and administrative expenses? These seem necessary, but is there a way to reduce them without impacting operations?

Manu: Absolutely. **G&A expenses** are essential for keeping your business running but don't contribute directly to sales or production. For TechZone, this might include office supplies, administrative salaries, accounting fees, and insurance.

Here's how you can manage G&A expenses:

- **Automate Routine Tasks**: Consider automating repetitive administrative tasks, like payroll or data entry. This reduces the time spent on manual work and can lower costs in the long run.

- **Streamline Office Supplies**: Only order essential office supplies in bulk, which often comes with discounts. Reduce paper usage by going digital where possible. Small savings add up over time.

- **Outsource Non-Core Functions**: For tasks like accounting, IT support, or human resources, outsourcing may be more cost-effective than hiring in-house. For TechZone, if your accounting needs are simple, you could use a part-time accountant or an online service.

Vinu: That makes sense. So, even with essential costs, we can still look for ways to streamline and reduce unnecessary spending.

Manu: Exactly. By optimizing G&A expenses, TechZone can free up cash for other areas that directly contribute to growth, like product development or marketing.

5. Creating an Expense Management Strategy

Vinu: This has been really helpful, Manu. But how do I bring all these strategies together into an overall expense management approach?

Manu: Great question! Here are a few steps to create an expense management strategy for TechZone:

- **Categorize Expenses**: Start by grouping expenses into categories like direct, indirect, selling, and G&A. This makes it easier to track and evaluate spending in each area.

- **Set Budgets for Each Category**: Allocate budgets based on past spending patterns and business goals. Track each category monthly to ensure you're staying within limits. If you see higher-than-expected spending, review and adjust accordingly.

- **Monitor Regularly**: Use accounting software to track expenses and generate reports. Monthly reviews help you spot trends, track overspending, and identify areas for cost reduction.

- **Review Vendor Contracts Annually**: Renegotiate with suppliers and service providers regularly. You might find better deals or discounts for long-term commitments.

- **Involve Your Team**: Educate your team on expense management goals and encourage cost-saving practices. Everyone can contribute to reducing costs by making small changes, like conserving energy or reducing waste.

Vinu: I like the idea of involving the team. If everyone understands the importance of managing expenses, we can all work together to make TechZone more efficient.

Manu: Exactly. Expense management is a team effort, and when everyone's on board, it's much easier to cut costs and improve profit margins.

Vinu: Thanks, Manu. I'm beginning to see how focusing on these different types of expenses can make a big difference. We'll start tracking each category and work on implementing these strategies.

Manu: You're welcome, Vinu! Managing expenses effectively can have a direct impact on your bottom line, making TechZone more profitable and sustainable. Now that we've covered expense management, let's move on to **understanding financial statements** in the next chapter. This will help you see how all these expenses affect the bigger financial picture.

3.6 Optimizing Labor Costs for Maximum Profitability

Vinu: Manu, I've noticed that labor costs make up a significant portion of our expenses at TechZone. How can we manage these costs better without compromising on quality or employee satisfaction?

Manu: That's a great observation, Vinu! Managing labor costs is crucial, as it directly impacts your profitability. It's not just about reducing costs but about maximizing the value you get from your employees. When done well, labor cost management can actually boost productivity and profit margins. Let's go over some strategies to help you optimize these costs while keeping employees engaged and motivated.

1. Enhancing Employee Performance

Vinu: Improving employee performance sounds like a good place to start. How does that help with labor costs?

Manu: When employees are performing well, they're more productive, which means you get more output for the same cost. For TechZone, this could mean higher sales, better customer service, or faster production times. Here's how to boost performance:

- **Set Clear Goals**: Make sure each employee understands their role and responsibilities. Set measurable goals so they know what's expected. For instance, if your sales team has monthly targets, they're more likely to focus on meeting those targets, which drives productivity.

- **Regular Training**: Invest in skills training to improve efficiency. For example, if your tech support team is well-trained, they can resolve customer issues faster, leading to better customer satisfaction and fewer callbacks.

- **Provide Constructive Feedback**: Regular feedback helps employees stay on track. Recognize good performance and address areas for improvement. When employees feel supported, they're more likely to stay motivated and productive.

Vinu: So by investing in training and setting clear goals, we're improving their efficiency, which means we're getting more value for the wages we're paying?

Manu: Exactly! The more productive your employees are, the lower your labor costs per unit of output. It's all about maximizing the return on your labor investment.

2. Implementing Performance-Based Incentives

Vinu: I like the idea of motivating employees, but won't incentives increase costs? How do they help with managing labor costs?

Manu: That's a good question, Vinu. While incentives may add to costs in the short term, they can significantly boost productivity and profitability in the long run. For example, if TechZone sets up performance-based incentives, like bonuses for meeting sales targets or completing projects ahead of schedule, it motivates employees to work harder and more efficiently.

Here's how incentives help manage labor costs:

- **Boosts Productivity**: When employees know they'll be rewarded for high performance, they tend to be more focused and motivated. This leads to increased productivity, which means you're getting more output for your labor costs.

- **Reduces Turnover**: Offering incentives can improve job satisfaction and reduce turnover. When employees stay longer, you save on the costs associated with hiring and training new staff.

- **Aligns Goals**: Performance-based incentives encourage employees to focus on what matters most to the business. For TechZone, this could mean offering incentives tied to customer satisfaction ratings or sales growth, both of which impact profitability.

Vinu: That makes sense. So even if we're spending a bit more on incentives, the overall gains in productivity and reduced hiring costs make it worthwhile?

Manu: Absolutely. Incentives are an investment in your team's performance. When structured well, they pay for themselves many times over by driving results that contribute directly to profit.

3. Turning Employees into Profit Centers

Vinu: You mentioned making employees into profit centers. How do we achieve that?

Manu: Turning employees into profit centers means empowering them to directly contribute to revenue or cost savings. This approach helps them understand their role in the company's success and encourages them to think like business owners. Here are a few ways to make it happen:

- **Set Revenue Goals**: For customer-facing roles, such as sales or customer support, set goals tied to revenue. For example, TechZone's sales team can focus on upselling or cross-selling products to boost revenue. You can even set targets for customer support to reduce refunds by resolving issues on the first call.

- **Encourage Cost-Saving Initiatives**: For operational roles, encourage employees to find ways to cut costs. If your production team finds ways to reduce material waste, offer them a share of the savings as a reward. At TechZone, if your warehouse team figures out how to pack items more efficiently, reducing packaging costs, they're directly contributing to profit.

- **Share Financial Goals with the Team**: When employees know what the business is aiming for, they're more likely to take ownership. If TechZone is trying to reduce expenses by 10%, share this goal with your team and ask for their ideas. You'd be surprised at how motivated they can be to find solutions.

Vinu: That's interesting! By setting revenue and cost-saving goals, we're basically giving employees a stake in the business's success. They'll be more invested in finding ways to save money or increase sales.

Manu: Exactly, Vinu! When employees see the impact of their efforts on the company's bottom line, they're more motivated to contribute. It's a win-win for both the business and the team.

4. Managing Overtime and Scheduling Efficiently

Vinu: Overtime costs seem to add up quickly. How can we manage labor scheduling better to avoid this?

Manu: Overtime can definitely eat into profits if not managed well. The key is **efficient scheduling**. For TechZone, look at your busiest times and schedule shifts accordingly to ensure you have enough coverage without needing overtime. Here's how:

- **Plan Schedules in Advance**: By planning ahead, you can avoid last-minute overtime needs. Use software to forecast demand and create schedules that align with TechZone's busiest hours.

- **Cross-Train Employees**: Train employees to handle multiple roles so they can fill in where needed. If someone on the production line can also help with packaging during peak times, it reduces the need to hire extra staff or pay overtime.

- **Limit Overtime Hours**: Set policies that limit the amount of overtime allowed. Encourage managers to seek alternatives, like shifting tasks to the next day if they're not urgent or reallocating team members as needed.

Vinu: So by being proactive with scheduling and training employees to take on different roles, we can reduce unnecessary overtime?

Manu: Exactly. Proactive scheduling not only helps you avoid overtime costs but also keeps your team working at a sustainable pace.

5. Using Technology to Track and Optimize Labor Costs

Vinu: Are there tools that can help us manage labor costs more effectively?

Manu: Absolutely! **Labor management software** can help TechZone track productivity, monitor attendance, and manage payroll. Here are a few ways technology can optimize labor costs:

- **Automated Time Tracking**: Use software to track employee hours accurately. This reduces the chances of overpaying for hours worked and helps ensure employees are paid fairly.

- **Productivity Tracking**: Some software allows you to track productivity per employee, which is useful for identifying high performers and areas where efficiency can be improved.

- **Scheduling Tools**: Many tools offer scheduling features that allow you to set shifts based on demand, reducing idle time and unnecessary overtime. You can adjust schedules based on real-time needs, which keeps labor costs in check.

Vinu: It sounds like using software can help us monitor labor costs closely and make adjustments in real-time.

Manu: Exactly, Vinu. The right tools make it easy to see where your labor costs are going and find ways to optimize them. It helps you maintain control over costs while ensuring you have the right people in the right roles.

6. Avoiding Common Labor Cost Pitfalls

Vinu: What are some mistakes I should watch out for when it comes to labor costs?

Manu: Here are a few common pitfalls to avoid:

- **Underestimating Training Needs**: Skipping training to save costs often backfires, as untrained employees tend to work slower and make more mistakes. For TechZone, invest in training to ensure employees are productive and efficient from day one.

- **Overstaffing**: Having too many employees on shift when they're not needed increases costs without adding value. Monitor demand trends and adjust staffing accordingly to avoid this.

- **Ignoring Employee Engagement**: Employees who feel undervalued or disconnected tend to be less productive. Offer recognition, create growth opportunities, and involve them in business goals. Engaged employees are more motivated and contribute to profitability.

- **Lack of Performance Reviews**: Regular reviews help employees stay on track and improve where needed. For TechZone, schedule reviews at least twice a year to assess performance, set goals, and address any issues.

Vinu: I'll definitely keep these in mind. It's clear that managing labor costs goes beyond just wages—it's about creating an environment where employees are productive, motivated, and aligned with our goals.

Manu: Exactly! When you manage labor costs strategically, you're not only reducing expenses but also creating a team that's engaged, efficient, and ready to drive TechZone's success.

Vinu: Thanks, Manu. This conversation has helped me understand how to manage labor costs in a way that actually adds value. I'm excited to start applying these strategies.

Manu: You're welcome, Vinu! Labor is one of the biggest costs for any business, but with the right approach, it can also become one of your biggest assets. By focusing on performance, incentives, scheduling, and employee engagement, you're setting TechZone up for better profitability.

3.7 Mastering Overall Cashflow Management

Vinu: Manu, we've covered receivables and payables in depth. I can see how managing both carefully helps with cash flow, but I'm still not sure how to keep the bigger picture in mind. How do I bring everything together for a solid cash flow management strategy?

Manu: Great question, Vinu! Cash flow management is all about making sure you have enough money coming in to cover the money going out—and ideally, a bit left over for growth. When you're managing both receivables and payables effectively, you're already taking big steps toward better cash flow. But there are other areas to focus on too, like budgeting, forecasting, and maintaining cash reserves. Let's walk through how to bring all these elements together for TechZone.

1. Understanding Cash Flow Cycles

Vinu: I've heard about cash flow cycles, but how do I know what TechZone's cycle looks like?

Manu: The **cash flow cycle**, or **cash conversion cycle (CCC)**, shows how long it takes for cash to move through the business—from buying inventory to receiving payment from customers. Essentially, it's the time between paying your suppliers and getting paid by your customers. We have already discussed about this. Hope you remember!

By reducing the time it takes to sell inventory and collect payments, and by taking full advantage of payment terms, you can shorten TechZone's cash flow cycle and keep cash flowing more steadily.

Vinu: That makes sense. So if I shorten the time it takes to sell inventory and collect payments while using the full payment terms with suppliers, I can improve cash flow?

Manu: Exactly. Optimizing each part of the cycle gives you more control over cash flow and keeps the business running smoothly.

2. Creating a Cash Flow Forecast

Vinu: How do I predict cash flow? Sometimes it feels like there are just too many variables.

Manu: It can feel that way, but a **cash flow forecast** helps you anticipate future cash needs based on expected income and expenses. We talked about it in Forecasting already. Start with a simple projection for the next three months, then extend it to six or twelve months as you become more comfortable.

Once you've estimated your cash flow, review it regularly. This way, you can see if there are any cash shortages coming up and plan ahead.

Vinu: So, it's like creating a roadmap for TechZone's finances. If I see a potential cash shortfall, I can take action before it becomes an issue?

Manu: Exactly, Vinu. A cash flow forecast helps you stay proactive rather than reactive, so you can avoid surprises and make well-informed decisions.

3. Maintaining a Cash Reserve

Vinu: We usually reinvest profits back into the business, but is it better to keep some cash aside as a reserve?

Manu: Absolutely. A **cash reserve** acts as a financial cushion, covering you in case of unexpected expenses or slow sales periods. For example, if TechZone has a slower sales month or needs an urgent equipment repair, the cash reserve helps cover those costs without disrupting day-to-day operations.

Aim to set aside enough cash to cover three to six months of operating expenses. Start small if needed and gradually build up the reserve over time. Having this cushion gives you peace of mind and flexibility to handle surprises.

Vinu: That's a good idea. We'll start building a cash reserve so we're better prepared for any unforeseen expenses.

Manu: Great! A cash reserve is like insurance—it's there when you need it, helping you avoid taking on unnecessary debt or dipping into funds meant for growth.

4. Avoiding Cash Flow Mistakes

Vinu: What are some common cash flow mistakes that I should avoid?

Manu: There are a few pitfalls to watch out for when managing cash flow:

- **Overestimating Revenue**: It's easy to be optimistic about sales, but if you overestimate, you may end up with less cash than expected. Be conservative with projections and plan based on realistic expectations.

- **Ignoring Small Expenses**: Little costs can add up quickly. For example, if TechZone frequently buys small office supplies, those can add up over time. Track these costs, so you're not surprised by them at the end of the month.

- **Overextending Credit**: Offering customers too much credit can tie up cash. Make sure payment terms are clear and keep an eye on overdue accounts.

- **Underestimating Tax Liabilities**: Taxes can have a big impact on cash flow. Set aside funds for taxes regularly so you're not caught off guard by a large bill.

- **Not Reviewing Financial Statements**: Regularly reviewing cash flow statements helps you understand where money is coming from and going. This helps you spot trends and identify potential cash flow issues early.

Vinu: Those are helpful tips. I'll keep an eye on those areas to make sure we're not falling into any traps.

Manu: Great! Avoiding these common mistakes will help you maintain steady cash flow and give you more control over TechZone's finances.

5. Using Technology to Improve Cash Flow Management

Vinu: We're still handling some of our finances manually. Would using software help with cash flow management?

Manu: Absolutely. Cash flow management software can automate much of the process, helping you track receivables, payables, and overall cash flow in real-time. Here's how it can benefit TechZone:

- **Automated Invoicing and Reminders**: Software can automatically send invoices and follow-up reminders, speeding up collections and reducing late payments.

- **Cash Flow Forecasting**: Many tools offer forecasting features, allowing you to see future cash flow projections. This gives you a clearer picture of what's coming and lets you plan accordingly.

- **Expense Tracking**: By tracking expenses in real-time, you can quickly spot areas where costs are higher than expected and make adjustments.

- **Integration with Banking**: Software often connects directly with your bank accounts, so you get an up-to-date view of cash inflows and outflows. This makes it easy to monitor cash balances and make informed decisions.

Vinu: That sounds really useful. So, automating some of these processes would give us more accurate data and save time too?

Manu: Exactly. Automation reduces human error and ensures you always have an accurate view of your cash position. It makes cash flow management easier and more reliable.

Vinu: Thanks, Manu. I feel like I have a much better understanding of how to keep TechZone's cash flow in check. It's clear that managing receivables, payables, and cash flow together creates a solid foundation.

Manu: You're welcome, Vinu! Cash flow management is the heartbeat of a healthy business. When you're managing cash well, you're prepared for both challenges and opportunities. Now that we've laid this foundation, let's move on to **budgeting and financial planning** in the next chapter. It will help you set goals, allocate resources, and keep TechZone on track for growth.

Vinu: Perfect! Let's get started on that.

Chapter 4 - Cost and Profitability Management

4.1 Cost Control and Efficiency

Vinu: Manu, I wish to know more about "cost control". I know it's important for **TechZone**, but I feel like there's more to it than just cutting expenses. Can we dive deeper into what it really means and how I can use it to improve **TechZone's** profitability?

Manu: Ah, you're absolutely right, Vinu! **Cost control** isn't just about slashing expenses; it's about being smart with your spending and ensuring every rupee you spend is helping you grow or operate efficiently. Think of it as optimizing every part of your business so you're not wasting resources. It's the difference between running a business that's just getting by and running one that's truly profitable and sustainable.

Let's explore how you can monitor and optimize **TechZone's** costs in a way that not only preserves profitability but also improves efficiency.

Manu: Imagine this: **TechZone** is growing, your sales are doing well, but somehow, profits aren't increasing as much as you expected. One of the culprits could be rising **operating costs** eating into your profit margins. Proper **cost control** ensures that while your business grows, you're keeping costs in check so that more of your revenue turns into profit.

It's about finding that balance—investing in growth while avoiding unnecessary expenses. Without this, you could end up overspending in areas that don't bring value to your business.

Vinu: So, it's about spending in the right places to keep costs from ballooning and ensuring I'm maximizing profits, right?

Manu: Exactly. And when you monitor and optimize your costs, you're doing more than just keeping the business afloat—you're driving it towards **profitability** and **efficiency**. Let's break it down.

Manu: Cost control doesn't mean cutting costs across the board. You need to focus on areas where you can eliminate waste without sacrificing quality or performance. Here's where **TechZone** can start:

1. Operating Expenses (OPEX):

These include rent, utilities, salaries, and other day-to-day costs. For **TechZone**, this could be the cost of running your office, paying staff, and managing logistics. You need to make sure these expenses are necessary and well-managed.

Example: Let's say **TechZone** is spending ₹1,50,000 on marketing every month. If that's not generating enough sales, it's time to review and possibly reallocate those funds to channels that work better, such as targeted digital ads.

2. Cost of Goods Sold (COGS):

This is the direct cost of producing or purchasing the goods you sell. If **TechZone** is spending ₹7,00,000 a month on purchasing gadgets, you could look into negotiating better prices with suppliers, buying in bulk for discounts, or switching to more cost-effective suppliers without compromising on quality.

3. Production or Inventory Costs:

If you hold too much inventory or produce more than you can sell, you're tying up cash unnecessarily. Look at ways to optimize inventory management, such as reducing overstocking or using just-in-time inventory to lower storage costs.

4. Administrative Costs:

These include expenses like software subscriptions, office supplies, and travel costs. For **TechZone**, if you're paying for software you don't use regularly or traveling unnecessarily for meetings that could be done online, those are costs you can cut without impacting the business.

Vinu: Okay, that makes sense. So, it's not about cutting costs randomly, but focusing on areas where I can reduce waste or optimize spending without hurting the business.

Manu: Exactly! It's about **optimizing** rather than just reducing. Every cost should be contributing to the growth and efficiency of **TechZone**. Now, let's look at **how** you can do that.

Manu: Once you know where to focus, the next step is figuring out **how** to control costs effectively. Here's how you can do that for **TechZone**:

1. Set Benchmarks and Track Spending:

Start by setting **benchmarks** for each type of expense. For instance, if you know that rent should only be 10% of your total operating costs, but it's currently 15%, that's a sign you might need to renegotiate your lease or find a more cost-effective office space.

You should also track spending closely. For **TechZone**, you could use accounting software to keep tabs on your expenses and identify areas where spending is creeping up unnecessarily.

2. Regularly Review Costs:

Don't just set and forget. Regularly review all your expenses to make sure they're still necessary and offering value. For example, if **TechZone** has been spending a lot on a certain supplier for two years, it might be time to shop around for better prices. You could also renegotiate terms, like asking for longer payment periods or bulk discounts.

3. Embrace Technology:

Use technology to your advantage. For instance, automate processes like invoicing, payroll, and inventory management. This not only reduces administrative costs but also cuts down on human error and saves time. If **TechZone** is manually tracking inventory, switching to an automated system could help you reduce errors and better manage stock levels, saving money.

4. Train and Empower Employees:

Often, inefficiencies come from how tasks are performed. Training your staff to be more efficient in their roles can reduce waste and improve productivity. For example, if **TechZone's** sales team is struggling with converting leads, investing in training to improve their skills can lead to higher sales without increasing marketing spend.

5. Energy Efficiency and Waste Reduction:

Think about ways to make **TechZone** more energy-efficient. Simple things like switching to energy-saving bulbs, cutting down on printing, or recycling materials can lead to long-term cost savings. These small changes can add up significantly over time.

Vinu: So, it's a mix of tracking, reviewing, and then optimizing through better processes and maybe even using technology to cut down unnecessary expenses.

Manu: Exactly, Vinu! And once you get into the habit of reviewing your costs regularly, it becomes easier to spot opportunities for savings or areas where things might be getting out of control.

Vinu: I see how cutting unnecessary costs helps, but how does that actually drive **profitability** for TechZone?

Manu: Great question! When you control costs effectively, you **increase your profit margins**. Here's how it works:

1. Lower Costs = Higher Margins:

Every rupee you save on operating costs, production, or administrative expenses directly boosts your bottom line. For example, if **TechZone** manages to reduce COGS by ₹50,000 a month through better supplier negotiations, that's ₹50,000 more in profit each month without having to increase sales.

2. Cost Control Enables Strategic Investment:

When you have savings from cost control, you can reinvest those savings into growth areas. For example, if you save ₹2,00,000 a year by optimizing your inventory, you could reinvest that into marketing or developing new products, which further drives growth.

3. Improves Cash Flow:

Controlling costs also improves your **cash flow**. You'll have more money available to cover short-term needs like payroll or rent, reducing the need for external borrowing. Better cash flow means more financial stability for **TechZone**.

4. Helps Navigate Tough Times:

In times of market uncertainty or slow sales, having good cost control practices can help keep your business afloat. When revenue drops, businesses that have a handle on their costs are better positioned to survive downturns.

Vinu: So, controlling costs isn't just about saving money—it's about creating opportunities for growth and making sure **TechZone** is more profitable and resilient.

Manu: Exactly! Cost control, when done right, frees up resources, improves your margins, and allows you to grow without taking on unnecessary risks.

Vinu: What kind of problems can I avoid if I get good at controlling costs?

Manu: There are several key issues you can avoid:

1. Profit Erosion:

Without proper cost control, rising expenses can eat into your profits, even if your sales are growing. For TechZone, this might mean that while sales are strong, increased operating costs could be quietly eroding your profit margins.

2. Cash Flow Problems:

Uncontrolled expenses can lead to cash shortages, especially if payments to suppliers, staff, or rent pile up. Proper cost control ensures that you always have enough cash on hand to meet your obligations.

3. Inability to Invest in Growth:

When your costs are high, you have less flexibility to invest in new products, marketing, or expansion. By managing costs well, **TechZone** can free up cash for strategic investments.

4. Becoming Non-Competitive:

If your costs are too high, you may have to charge higher prices, making your products less competitive in the market. Effective cost control allows you to offer competitive prices while still maintaining healthy profit margins.

Vinu: Got it. So, controlling costs helps me avoid cash flow issues, keeps my profits from shrinking, and gives me room to invest in the growth of **TechZone**.

Manu: Exactly! When you master cost control, you're not just saving money—you're building a **sustainable** and **profitable** business that's ready for whatever challenges or opportunities come your way.

4.2 Break Even Analysis

Vinu: Manu, I've been hearing people talk about the **break-even point** and how important it is for understanding profitability, but it still feels like a vague concept to me. Can we break it down? I feel like there's something deeper I need to understand here for **TechZone**.

Manu: Ah, you've hit on one of the most fundamental financial concepts, Vinu! Knowing your **break-even point** is like having a map for your business—it shows you exactly when you stop just surviving and start **thriving**. Think of it as the moment where the effort you've put in starts paying off because your revenue finally covers all costs, and everything beyond that is pure **profit**.

Let's not just talk theory—let's make this **real** for **TechZone**.

Manu: The **break-even point** is the point at which your **revenue** equals your **total costs**—both **fixed** and **variable**. At this point, you're neither making a profit nor a loss; you've simply covered all your expenses. After this point, every additional rupee in revenue goes towards profit.

For **TechZone**, this would be the number of gadgets you need to sell to cover your **fixed costs** (like rent, salaries, etc.) and your **variable costs** (like the cost of goods sold, packaging, etc.).

Vinu: Okay, that makes sense. So, once I hit the **break-even point**, I'm no longer just covering costs—I'm actually making a profit?

Manu: Exactly. Before you reach the break-even point, you're still playing catch-up—trying to cover what it costs to run the business. After you hit that point, all the sales you make contribute directly to profit.

How to Calculate the Break-Even Point

Manu: Let's get practical. To calculate the **break-even point** for **TechZone**, we need two main pieces of information:

1. Fixed Costs: These are the costs that don't change regardless of how many gadgets you sell. For **TechZone**, let's say your monthly fixed costs include:

Rent: ₹50,000

Salaries: ₹1,00,000

Utilities: ₹20,000

So, your **total fixed costs** are ₹1,70,000 per month.

2. Variable Costs per Unit: These are the costs associated with producing and selling each gadget. Let's assume:

Cost of Goods Sold (COGS): ₹3,000 per gadget

Packaging and shipping: ₹500 per gadget

So, your **total variable cost** per unit is ₹3,500.

3. Selling Price per Unit: Let's say you sell each gadget for ₹5,000.

The formula for the **break-even point in units** is:

Break-even point (units) = Fixed Costs / (Selling Price per Unit−Variable Cost per Unit)

Let's apply this to **TechZone**:

Break-even point = ₹1,70,000 / (₹5,000−₹3,500) =₹1,70,000 - ₹1,500 =113.33 units.

So, **TechZone** needs to sell **114 gadgets** per month to break even.

Vinu: Wow, that's clearer now! So, if I sell 114 gadgets in a month, I'm just covering my costs. Every gadget after that is contributing to profit?

Manu: Exactly! Once you sell 114 gadgets, you've covered all your costs. After that, each additional sale is pure profit (after covering the variable costs of production, of course).

Why is Knowing the Break-Even Point Important?

Manu: Now that we know the **break-even point**, let's talk about why it's so important for **TechZone**:

1. Sets Revenue Targets:

Knowing your break-even point gives you a clear sales target. You know that if you sell less than 114 gadgets, you'll be operating at a loss. If you want to hit profitability, you'll need to aim for sales **above** that break-even number.

2. Helps with Pricing Strategy:

Understanding the break-even point also helps you evaluate whether your **pricing** is right. For example, if your break-even point seems too high (you need to sell too many units to break even), it might mean your **margins** are too low, and you should consider raising your prices or finding ways to reduce costs.

3. Informs Decision-Making:

It helps with big decisions—whether it's launching a new product, expanding into a new market, or even increasing operational costs. For **TechZone**, knowing that you need to sell 114 gadgets just to break even might make you rethink hiring additional staff or moving to a larger office space unless you're confident in increasing sales.

4. Manages Risk:

Understanding your break-even point also gives you a buffer to manage risks. For example, if a supplier increases prices or sales drop unexpectedly, you know exactly how many units you need to sell to stay afloat.

Vinu: That makes sense. It's not just a number—it's a benchmark to guide decisions. So, knowing this can also help me plan for growth, right?

Manu: Absolutely! Once you know your break-even point, you can set sales goals **beyond** it to plan for profitability and growth.

Manu: Now, let's talk about how **profitability** works **after** you pass the break-even point. Once **TechZone** sells more than 114 gadgets, each sale contributes to profit. The more gadgets you sell, the more profit you generate, provided your variable costs don't change significantly.

To calculate your **profit**, you can use the following formula:

Profit = (Total Sales−Total Variable Costs)−Fixed Costs

Let's assume **TechZone** sells **150 gadgets** this month. Here's how that breaks down:

1. Total Sales:

₹5,000 (price per gadget) × 150 gadgets = ₹7,50,000.

2. Total Variable Costs:

₹3,500 (variable cost per gadget) × 150 gadgets = ₹5,25,000.

3. Profit Calculation:

Profit = (₹7,50,000 - ₹5,25,000) - ₹1,70,000 (fixed costs)

   = ₹2,25,000 - ₹1,70,000

   = ₹55,000.

So, by selling **150 gadgets**, **TechZone** would make a profit of ₹55,000.

Vinu: That's awesome! So, now I know exactly how many gadgets I need to sell to cover my costs and how much profit I'll make if I sell more.

Manu: Exactly! Understanding this gives you the power to **strategically plan** how to push past your break-even point and maximize profit.

Vinu: Is there a way to **lower** the break-even point, or should I just focus on selling more gadgets?

Manu: Good question! There are two key ways to lower your break-even point:

1. Increase Your Selling Price:

If you can increase your **selling price** without losing customers, you'll reach your break-even point faster. For TechZone, if you raise the price of each gadget from ₹5,000 to ₹5,500, your break-even point would drop.

Let's calculate:

Break-even point =₹1,70,000 / (₹5,500−₹3,500)

$$= ₹1,70,000 / ₹2,000$$

$$=85 \text{ gadgets}$$

Now, you'd only need to sell **85 gadgets** to break even.

2. Reduce Your Fixed or Variable Costs:

Reducing costs also helps. For example, if you negotiate lower rent or salaries, your fixed costs drop, lowering your break-even point. Similarly, if you can negotiate with suppliers to lower the cost of each gadget, your variable costs will go down, which also reduces the number of units you need to sell to break even.

Vinu: So, I could either raise prices or lower costs to make it easier to break even?

Manu: Exactly! And once you lower your break-even point, you'll start making a profit sooner and have more flexibility to grow.

Vinu: What happens if I don't focus on my break-even point?

Manu: If you ignore your break-even point, you're essentially operating in the dark. Here's what can go wrong:

1. Underestimating Costs:

Without understanding your break-even point, you might underestimate how much revenue you need to cover your costs, leading to financial shortfalls.

2. Overestimating Profit:

Some businesses think they're making a profit because they're generating revenue, but if they haven't reached the break-even point, they're still losing money.

3. Poor Decision-Making:

Without a clear understanding of when you'll break even, you might make poor decisions—like expanding too early or taking on unnecessary costs that make it even harder to break even.

4. Cash Flow Problems:

Not reaching your break-even point consistently can lead to cash flow issues, as you're spending more than you're bringing in. This could result in the need for loans or other external financing to keep the business running.

Vinu: I see. It's not just a concept—it's a vital tool for decision-making and ensuring **TechZone** is running profitably.

Manu: Exactly! Once you master the **break-even point** and how it relates to your profitability, you'll have a powerful tool to guide your business decisions and drive **TechZone** toward long-term success.

4.3 Measuring Return on Marketing Investments

Vinu: Manu, I've been investing quite a bit in marketing to get TechZone's name out there, but I'm struggling to understand how to measure the actual returns. I know some benefits are hard to pin down, but is there a way to really know if our marketing spend is paying off?

Manu: That's a great question, Vinu! Measuring marketing ROI is essential for making sure you're spending wisely and focusing on the channels that give the best returns. You're right that it can be tricky, especially with traditional marketing, but there are still ways to gauge effectiveness. Let's look at some ways you can measure returns for both traditional and digital marketing.

Traditional Marketing ROI

Vinu: I get that digital marketing is more measurable, but what about our traditional marketing? How do we measure things like TV or radio ads?

Manu: Traditional marketing is tougher to track directly, but there are a few key metrics that can give you a sense of its impact. Let's start with **incremental sales**. When you run a traditional marketing campaign, like a TV ad, you can look at the increase in sales during and after the campaign compared to a previous period. If sales go up, you can attribute part of that increase to the campaign.

Vinu: So, it's about tracking sales patterns over time and seeing if there's a lift?

Manu: Exactly. Another useful metric is **Cost Per Acquisition (CPA)**, which tells you how much it costs to acquire a new customer from each campaign. For example, if you spend ₹50,000 on a radio ad and acquire 100 new customers, your CPA is ₹500.

Vinu: That makes sense. What about things like brand awareness or foot traffic? We can't measure those directly, can we?

Manu: For things like **foot traffic** or **brand awareness**, you can use proxies. For example, you could monitor foot traffic in your stores during the campaign. Or, use surveys to ask customers if they heard about TechZone from a specific ad.

Another option is to use **coupon codes or special offers** in your traditional marketing. For example, if you run a print ad, include a unique code. That way, when customers redeem the offer, you know exactly where they came from.

Vinu: So, it's about getting creative and finding ways to track impact indirectly?

Manu: Exactly. Traditional marketing requires a bit of indirect tracking, but with methods like unique codes and customer surveys, you can get a pretty good sense of what's working.

Digital Marketing ROI

Vinu: Now, I assume digital marketing is a lot more straightforward to track?

Manu: It definitely is. Digital marketing offers more precise tracking tools, which makes measuring ROI easier. One of the key metrics is **Return on Ad Spend (ROAS)**. This measures how much revenue you generate for every rupee you spend on advertising.

For example, if you spend ₹10,000 on a Google Ads campaign and it generates ₹30,000 in sales, your ROAS is 3:1. That means for every rupee you spent, you got three rupees back.

Vinu: That's simple enough. So, ROAS is basically a direct way to measure the return. What else should I track?

Manu: Another important metric is **Customer Acquisition Cost (CAC)**, which shows you the cost to acquire each new customer. For instance, if you spend ₹20,000 on Facebook ads and acquire 200 customers, your CAC is

₹100 per customer. It's helpful to compare this with the lifetime value of the customer to see if you're spending sustainably.

Vinu: And what about metrics for things like website clicks or conversion rates?

Manu: Great point. **Conversion Rate** and **Click-Through Rate (CTR)** are crucial for understanding how well your digital ads perform.

- **Conversion Rate** shows the percentage of people who take a desired action, like making a purchase. If 100 people click on your ad and 10 make a purchase, your conversion rate is 10%.

- **CTR** measures how many people clicked on your ad out of the total who saw it. For example, if 1,000 people saw a TechZone ad and 50 clicked, your CTR is 5%.

These metrics let you see if your ad is effective at capturing attention and converting interest into action.

Vinu: Got it. And I've heard about lifetime value and comparing that with CAC. Is that something I should focus on?

Manu: Absolutely! **Lifetime Value (LTV)** shows you how much profit a customer generates over their entire relationship with TechZone. Compare LTV to CAC to ensure you're acquiring customers profitably.

For example, if TechZone's LTV is ₹10,000 and your CAC is ₹1,000, you're generating a solid return. Ideally, you want your LTV to be significantly higher than CAC to make sure you're gaining long-term value from each customer.

Blending Traditional and Digital Metrics

Vinu: Okay, so traditional marketing is a bit more indirect, while digital marketing is more precise. But how do I put it all together? If we're running campaigns on both TV and social media, how can I measure overall returns?

Manu: Good question! This is where **blended marketing ROI** comes into play. To get a high-level view of your total marketing effectiveness, you can combine revenue from all channels and divide it by your total marketing spend.

For example, if TechZone generates ₹500,000 in revenue from both traditional and digital campaigns, and your total marketing spend across all channels was ₹100,000, your blended marketing ROI is 5:1.

Blended Marketing ROI = (Total Revenue from Marketing / Total Marketing Spend)

Vinu: That gives me an overall picture. Are there any tools or specific ways to track offline actions, like calls or store visits, back to digital campaigns?

Manu: Yes, you can use **call tracking** for offline conversions. By setting up unique phone numbers for different campaigns, you can see how many calls and conversions each ad drives. For instance, if you run a billboard ad with a specific phone number, you can track how many calls it generates.

And for digital, **UTM parameters** on your links let you track where online traffic is coming from. This can help you see which digital channels are driving people to specific actions, like making a purchase or signing up for a newsletter.

Using Metrics for Ongoing Improvement

Vinu: This makes a lot more sense now. So, by tracking these metrics, I can see what's working and adjust our marketing spend accordingly. How often should I be reviewing these?

Manu: Ideally, you want to review digital metrics weekly or monthly to make adjustments quickly. For traditional campaigns, you might evaluate impact monthly or quarterly, as those results take a bit longer to see.

Vinu: And when I see what's working best, I can focus more resources on those channels?

Manu: Exactly, Vinu! By regularly reviewing both traditional and digital marketing metrics, you can optimize your spending, focus on the most effective channels, and ultimately drive better returns for TechZone. Over time, this will help you build a strong marketing strategy that delivers consistent growth.

Vinu: Thanks, Manu! This is really helpful. I feel like I have a clearer picture of how to measure marketing success and make informed decisions moving forward.

Manu: Glad to hear it, Vinu! With a strong understanding of these metrics, you'll be able to maximize the impact of TechZone's marketing investments and grow the business effectively.

4.4 Creating a Smart Discount Policy

Vinu: Manu, I've been thinking about running some promotions for TechZone to boost sales, especially during slower months. But I'm worried that offering discounts might cut into our profits. How do I know when it's okay to offer a discount without hurting our bottom line?

Manu: That's a great question, Vinu. Discounts can indeed be a powerful way to attract customers, but you have to be strategic about them. The key is to offer discounts that drive volume or attract new customers while ensuring that they don't significantly reduce your profit margins. Let's look at some scenarios where discounts can work in your favor.

1. Clearing Out Old Inventory

Manu: One situation where offering a discount makes sense is when you're trying to clear out old or excess inventory. If you've got products that aren't selling as quickly, discounting them can free up space for new stock and bring in cash that you can reinvest.

Vinu: That makes sense. So, if TechZone has a batch of gadgets that's just sitting there, I could run a discount to move that stock faster?

Manu: Exactly. You're reducing inventory carrying costs and bringing in revenue, even if it's at a lower margin. The important thing is that you're turning stagnant stock into cash, which can then be used to invest in newer, faster-moving products.

2. Attracting First-Time Customers

Vinu: What about offering discounts to bring in new customers? Is that a smart move?

Manu: Absolutely, as long as you're targeting first-time customers. Offering a one-time discount can help attract new buyers and build brand loyalty. For instance, you could offer a 10% discount for first-time TechZone customers. Once they've tried your products, they're more likely to return and make full-price purchases in the future.

Vinu: So, it's more about using discounts as a tool to introduce people to TechZone?

Manu: Exactly. The idea is to think of the discount as an investment in customer acquisition. You might take a small hit initially, but if you're gaining repeat customers, the long-term value they bring will more than make up for the initial discount.

3. Increasing Order Volume

Manu: Another smart way to use discounts is by encouraging larger purchases. Offering a discount for higher quantities or for hitting a specific order value can be an effective strategy. For example, you could offer a 5% discount for orders over ₹5,000 or a 10% discount for orders over ₹10,000.

Vinu: How does that help with profits?

Manu: Volume discounts work because they increase the overall order size. As long as you've priced the discount to maintain your margins, the higher volume can offset the lower per-unit profit. Plus, bulk orders often mean lower shipping and handling costs per unit, which can further improve profitability.

4. Boosting Sales During Off-Peak Times

Vinu: What about seasonal discounts or promotions during slower periods? Are they worthwhile?

Manu: Yes, offering discounts during off-peak times is a great way to keep cash flow steady throughout the year. For instance, if TechZone has slower sales in certain months, a limited-time promotion can drive traffic and maintain revenue levels. This helps keep your operations running smoothly, even during leaner periods.

Vinu: So, the goal is to maintain consistent cash flow, right?

Manu: Exactly. Think of it as balancing your sales. By using discounts to boost sales during slower months, you can keep your business running more smoothly and avoid drastic revenue fluctuations. Just be mindful of how deep the discounts are, so you're not sacrificing too much margin.

5. Building Customer Loyalty and Retention

Manu: Offering discounts as a way to reward loyal customers is another effective strategy. For instance, you could create a loyalty program where customers earn points on each purchase that can be redeemed for discounts. This not only encourages repeat business but also builds a stronger relationship with your customers.

Vinu: That sounds like a good way to keep customers coming back. How can I make sure it's profitable?

Manu: The key is to structure the loyalty program so that it doesn't eat into your profits too much. For example, offering a small discount or reward for every five purchases ensures customers come back, but you're still generating consistent sales. With TechZone, you might offer a ₹500 discount after a customer has spent ₹10,000. This encourages larger or repeat purchases while keeping your profits healthy.

6. Measuring the Impact of Discounts

Vinu: How do I track whether a discount is actually working to improve profits?

Manu: It's important to measure the effectiveness of each discount you offer. Here are a few ways you can track impact:

- **Sales Volume**: Track how many additional units you're selling as a result of the discount. If the discount significantly increases volume, it could be worth it.

- **Profit Margin**: Calculate the difference in profit margin before and after the discount. Make sure the discount doesn't push your margin too low to be sustainable.

- **Customer Acquisition and Retention**: Track how many new customers are making repeat purchases. If you're gaining loyal customers from an initial discount, it's adding long-term value.

- **Break-Even Analysis**: Calculate how many units you need to sell at the discounted price to break even. If you're selling more than the break-even amount, the discount is likely profitable.

Vinu: That sounds simple enough. So, as long as I'm tracking these metrics, I can adjust discounts based on what's actually working?

Manu: Exactly. Discounts are a powerful tool, but only when used strategically. By tracking these metrics, you'll know when a discount is driving profitable growth versus when it's cutting into margins too much.

Final Thoughts on a Smart Discount Policy

Vinu: Thanks, Manu. I feel like I have a better grasp on how to use discounts in a way that benefits TechZone without hurting profits.

Manu: You're welcome, Vinu! Remember, the key to a successful discount policy is using it as a tool to reach specific goals, whether it's clearing inventory, acquiring new customers, or building loyalty. Keep your margins in mind, track the results, and make adjustments as needed. With the right approach, discounts can help grow your business sustainably.

Vinu: Great! I'm excited to try these strategies and see how they work for TechZone.

Manu: You're on the right path, Vinu. Just stay mindful of your goals, keep an eye on your metrics, and you'll be well on your way to a profitable and effective discount strategy.

4.5 Understanding Pricing Strategies for Business Success

Manu: Vinu, pricing is one of the most powerful tools you have as a business owner. It directly impacts profitability, customer perception, and how competitive you are in the market. Developing a strong pricing strategy can make a big difference in how TechZone grows and thrives.

Vinu: I've always just set my prices based on what competitors are doing and added a little extra to cover costs. But I feel like there must be more to it. What should I consider when creating a pricing strategy?

Manu: You're right, there's a lot more to it! Let's break down a few key components of pricing strategies. We'll start with **competitive pricing models**, move into **cost structures**, and then look at **demand and pricing elasticity**. Each piece plays an important role in setting prices that attract customers while keeping your profits healthy.

1. Developing Competitive Pricing Models

Manu: First, it's important to know where you stand in the market. To do this, you need to analyze competitors, understand customer expectations, and decide on a pricing model that aligns with TechZone's brand positioning. Here are a few common pricing models:

- **Cost-Plus Pricing**: This is a straightforward model where you add a markup to your cost. For example, if it costs you ₹500 to produce a gadget and you want a 20% profit, you'd price it at ₹600. It ensures you cover costs while making a profit.

- **Value-Based Pricing**: Here, you set prices based on the perceived value to the customer. For instance, if TechZone has a high-quality, unique feature on its gadgets, you could price it higher than competitors because customers value that feature.

- **Penetration Pricing**: This is useful if you want to attract new customers or gain market share. You set a low initial price to draw people in, then raise the price later once they're loyal. Imagine launching a new product at a discounted rate to build a customer base.

- **Premium Pricing**: If your brand positions itself as high-quality or exclusive, you might go for premium pricing. Luxury brands use this strategy to signal status and exclusivity, so TechZone could consider this if you have unique, high-end products.

- **Dynamic Pricing**: Some businesses adjust prices based on demand, seasonality, or competitors' prices. This is popular in industries like travel and e-commerce. You might increase prices during peak shopping seasons or when demand for a gadget is high.

Vinu: So, it's not just about covering costs but also about how I want to position TechZone in the market?

Manu: Exactly. Pricing is part of your brand identity. For example, if you're positioning TechZone as innovative and premium, you might lean towards value-based or premium pricing. If you're trying to capture a large customer base quickly, penetration pricing could be a better fit.

2. Analyzing Cost Structures to Determine Profitable Pricing

Manu: Next, let's talk about costs. Understanding your cost structure is essential for setting prices that are profitable. Here's what you need to look at:

- **Direct and Indirect Costs**: Direct costs are tied directly to production, like materials and labor. Indirect costs, or overheads, are expenses like rent, utilities, and salaries. You need to factor in both to ensure your pricing covers all costs.

- **Breakeven Analysis**: This is about determining the minimum price needed to cover all your costs. Say your total monthly costs for TechZone are ₹1,00,000, and you sell a gadget for ₹1,000. You'd need to sell at least 100 gadgets just to cover your expenses.

- **Target Profit Margins**: Once you cover costs, you'll want to set a target profit. For example, if you want a 30% margin on each gadget, you'd price it accordingly.

- **Contribution Margin Analysis**: This helps you understand how much each sale contributes to fixed costs and profits after covering variable costs. It's useful for making decisions about pricing and cost-cutting.

Vinu: So, I need to get a handle on both fixed and variable costs, and then think about how much profit I want on top of that?

Manu: Yes, and it helps you see which products are the most profitable. For example, if you know that your latest gadget has a higher contribution margin, you might prioritize it over products with slimmer margins. It also helps with decisions like whether to discount a product or bundle it with another.

3. Understanding Market Demand and Pricing Elasticity

Manu: Now, let's talk about **market demand and pricing elasticity**. This is about understanding how sensitive your customers are to price changes and how that affects demand. Here are a few things to consider:

- **Demand Elasticity**: This measures how much demand changes with a change in price. If demand is elastic, a small change in price leads to a big change in sales. For example, if you lower the price of a basic TechZone gadget and sales surge, it means your customers are price-sensitive.
  On the other hand, inelastic demand means customers are less sensitive to price changes, so you could raise prices without seeing a big drop in sales. Luxury or unique products often have inelastic demand because customers are willing to pay more for them.

- **Price Experimentation**: Sometimes, it's helpful to test different price points to see how customers respond. You might try offering a gadget at ₹1,000 and then at ₹1,200 to see if demand remains strong. This can help you find the price that maximizes revenue.

- **Customer Segmentation**: Different customer segments have different price sensitivities. For example, budget-conscious customers might prefer lower-priced items, while premium customers look for quality and are willing to pay more. You can adjust pricing for each segment to capture as much value as possible.

- **Psychological Pricing**: This is about setting prices in a way that appeals to customers' psychology. For example, pricing something at ₹999 instead of ₹1,000 can make it feel more affordable. It's a small difference, but it can impact buying decisions.

Vinu: I hadn't thought about how price-sensitive customers can be. So, by understanding elasticity, I can set prices that align with their willingness to pay?

Manu: Exactly. For TechZone, if you know your high-end gadgets have inelastic demand, you could set a higher price. But for everyday gadgets, where customers are more price-sensitive, a lower price might drive more sales. This approach helps you capture the maximum value from each customer segment.

4. Common Mistakes to Avoid in Pricing Strategies

Vinu: This all makes a lot of sense. Are there any common pitfalls I should watch out for when setting prices?

Manu: Yes, here are a few common mistakes to avoid:

- **Ignoring Costs**: Some businesses set prices based on competitors without considering their own costs. Always ensure that your price covers all expenses and provides the profit margin you need.

- **Not Understanding Customer Value**: Pricing should reflect the value your product offers. If TechZone's gadgets have unique features, pricing too low could make customers question the quality. On the flip side, pricing too high when there's no added value could drive customers to competitors.

- **Overusing Discounts**: Offering frequent discounts can erode perceived value. If customers start expecting discounts, they may avoid buying at full price. Discounts should be used strategically, like to clear excess inventory or during seasonal sales.

- **Inflexible Pricing**: Failing to adjust prices based on market conditions can hurt profits. If demand rises or costs increase, don't be afraid to adjust your prices accordingly. Dynamic pricing is helpful in staying responsive to the market.

Vinu: These are really good points, especially about avoiding constant discounts. I see how important it is to think carefully about how each pricing decision affects TechZone's brand and profitability.

Manu: Exactly. With a well-thought-out pricing strategy, you're not only maximizing profits but also positioning TechZone in a way that attracts the right customers and builds long-term success. The goal is to balance what customers are willing to pay with the value TechZone provides and the costs you need to cover.

Vinu: Thanks, Manu. This has been incredibly helpful. I feel like I have a much clearer understanding of how to set prices strategically.

4.6 Understanding Customer Profitability Analysis

Manu: Vinu, as TechZone continues to grow, one area that can really help boost your profits is something called **Customer Profitability Analysis**. It's about figuring out which customers are bringing in the most profit and which ones might actually be costing you money.

Vinu: Interesting! I always thought every customer was valuable, as long as they're buying from us. Are you saying that's not always the case?

Manu: That's right. While every customer contributes to your revenue, not every customer contributes equally to your profits. Some customers generate high sales but also require a lot of support or frequent discounts, which cuts into your profit margins. Customer Profitability Analysis helps you identify which customers are most profitable so you can focus on them and improve your overall profitability.

Vinu: That makes sense. So, how do we start analyzing customer profitability at TechZone?

Manu: First, let's look at the cost of serving each customer. For TechZone, this would mean breaking down costs related to sales, customer service, returns, and any other expenses directly tied to your customers. Then, you'll compare these costs to the revenue each customer brings in. This will help you see which customers are truly profitable.

1. Analyzing Costs Per Customer

Vinu: Could you walk me through an example?

Manu: Of course! Let's say TechZone has two customers, **Customer A** and **Customer B**. Both customers generate ₹1,00,000 in sales per year. At first glance, they look equally valuable, right?

Vinu: Yes, they're bringing in the same revenue, so I'd assume they're both equally profitable.

Manu: But let's dig a little deeper. Customer A is pretty low-maintenance. They place large orders quarterly, rarely need support, and rarely return products. Now, Customer B, on the other hand, places smaller orders but more frequently, needs a lot of follow-up, and often asks for returns or exchanges. This means you're spending more on sales, customer service, and handling returns for Customer B.

Vinu: So, even though they're both bringing in the same sales, the costs for Customer B are much higher?

Manu: Exactly. Let's say the total costs associated with Customer A are ₹20,000 per year. But for Customer B, they're closer to ₹50,000. This means that after subtracting costs, **Customer A contributes ₹80,000 in profit**, while **Customer B only contributes ₹50,000**. Despite the same sales, Customer A is more profitable.

Vinu: Wow, I hadn't thought about it like that. So by understanding these costs, I can see which customers are more valuable in terms of profit, not just revenue.

2. Segmenting Customers by Profitability

Manu: That's exactly it, Vinu. Once you know which customers are most profitable, you can segment them and focus your efforts where they'll make the biggest impact. For example, you might group your customers into three categories:

- **High-Profit Customers**: These customers bring in strong revenue with minimal costs. For TechZone, this could be customers who place large orders, rarely need support, and pay on time.

- **Moderate-Profit Customers**: These customers bring in reasonable revenue but require moderate support or discounts. They're valuable, but you'll want to monitor their costs.

- **Low-Profit or Unprofitable Customers**: These customers may bring in high sales but have equally high costs. For instance, if a customer frequently returns items or always negotiates heavy discounts, they might fall into this category.

Vinu: So, by segmenting my customers, I can see where to invest more resources and where I might need to cut back?

Manu: Exactly. With this segmentation, you can tailor your approach. For high-profit customers, you might focus on building loyalty and increasing sales. For low-profit customers, you might reconsider offering frequent discounts or even limit the resources you allocate to them.

3. Using Customer Profitability Analysis to Improve Profits

Vinu: I can see how this analysis would help identify which customers to prioritize. But how does it directly improve profits for TechZone?

Manu: Customer Profitability Analysis gives you the information you need to optimize your customer strategy. Here's how it can help increase profits:

- **Increase Focus on High-Profit Customers**: By investing in your most profitable customers, you encourage repeat business and potentially increase their spending. For example, you could offer them loyalty programs or exclusive offers, which can lead to higher sales without increasing costs significantly.

- **Optimize Support Costs for Low-Profit Customers**: For customers who require a lot of support, you can create a streamlined service model or encourage them to use self-service options. For instance, if certain customers often need help with setup, TechZone could provide detailed guides or online tutorials instead of sending a technician each time.

- **Adjust Pricing or Terms**: For customers who are just on the edge of profitability, you might look at adjusting terms. For example, you could require minimum order quantities or reduce discounts. By tweaking these terms, you can make less profitable customers more valuable.

Vinu: So instead of just looking at revenue, I'm making decisions based on which customers actually help the business grow?

Manu: Exactly. It's about maximizing your resources where they'll have the greatest impact. By focusing on high-profit customers and adjusting how you handle lower-profit ones, you can significantly improve TechZone's overall profitability.

4. Common Mistakes to Avoid with Customer Profitability Analysis

Vinu: Are there any common pitfalls to watch out for when doing this kind of analysis?

Manu: Yes, a few mistakes can reduce the effectiveness of customer profitability analysis:

- **Only Focusing on Revenue**: Many businesses focus on top-line sales and assume high-revenue customers are always valuable. But as we've seen, high revenue doesn't always equal high profit. Be sure to factor in all related costs.

- **Neglecting Long-Term Potential**: Some customers may not be very profitable initially but have strong growth potential. Don't dismiss a customer purely based on current costs if there's an opportunity to build a profitable relationship over time.

- **Not Re-evaluating Regularly**: Customer profitability can change over time as customers' needs and behaviors evolve. Make this analysis a regular practice—quarterly or annually—to ensure you're always working with up-to-date information.

Vinu: I see. So it's important to keep updating this information so that I'm always focused on the right customers.

Manu: Exactly. This should be a part of your regular business analysis, not a one-time activity. As you collect more data, you'll gain deeper insights into which customers drive TechZone's growth and which ones may be holding it back.

Vinu: Thanks, Manu. This has been eye-opening. I can see how Customer Profitability Analysis can really help me make better decisions about where to focus and how to increase profits.

Manu: You're absolutely right, Vinu. When you understand which customers bring the most value, you're able to invest resources more effectively and build a more profitable business. And with this information, you're in a stronger position to make financial decisions across the board.

Chapter 5 - Financing and Debt Management

5.1 Understand the structure of debt and its impact on the business

Vinu: Manu, I've been thinking about taking out a loan to help grow **TechZone**, but I'm a bit nervous about debt. I've heard stories of businesses thriving with loans, but also horror stories of debt destroying companies. How do I know if it's the right move for **TechZone**?

Manu: Ah, Vinu, debt is like a double-edged sword—it can be a powerful tool when used wisely, but it can also be a ticking time bomb if not managed carefully. In **good times**, debt can help your business **grow faster** by providing the capital you need to expand, but in **bad times**, it can **weigh you down** and potentially kill your business if you can't keep up with the repayments.

Let's break down when it makes sense to take on debt, when you should avoid it, and what to do if debt starts becoming unmanageable.

Manu: In good times, debt can be a powerful lever for growth. Here's how it can help **TechZone**:

1. Accelerating Growth:

If business is booming and you need more capital to expand, debt can help you scale faster. For example, if **TechZone** needs to buy more inventory to meet rising demand or open a new store, a loan can provide the immediate funds you need without waiting to generate enough cash from sales.

2. Leveraging Opportunities:

Sometimes, opportunities come up that require quick action, like buying discounted stock in bulk or investing in new technology that can improve productivity. Debt can provide the capital to seize those opportunities before competitors do.

3. Maintaining Ownership:

Unlike equity financing, taking on debt doesn't dilute your ownership in **TechZone**. You get the funds you need while maintaining full control of your business.

Vinu: That sounds great. So, if I have a clear growth plan and the business is doing well, debt can help me grow faster without giving up any control?

Manu: Exactly. But you need to make sure that you're borrowing **responsibly** and have a solid plan for repaying the debt. And now, let's talk about the flip side—what happens in **bad times**.

Manu: In bad times, debt can become a huge burden. Here's how it can go wrong:

- **Cash Flow Strain**: When sales drop or costs rise unexpectedly, debt repayments can eat into your cash flow. If **TechZone** takes on too much debt and sales slow down, you could find yourself struggling to make the monthly payments, which could lead to late fees, higher interest rates, or even default.

- **Interest and Repayment Pressure:** Loans come with interest, and the longer you have the debt, the more you're paying in interest. If the business isn't doing well, you're stuck with **fixed payments** that don't go away, even if your cash flow dries up. This can lead to a vicious cycle of borrowing more to cover old debts.

- **Loss of Flexibility**: Debt limits your financial flexibility. When you're heavily in debt, you don't have the freedom to invest in growth opportunities or adapt to changing market conditions because your cash is tied up in loan repayments.

Vinu: So, in bad times, the debt that was supposed to help me grow could actually drag **TechZone** down, especially if sales fall and I can't keep up with the payments?

Manu: Exactly. Debt can feel like an anchor pulling you down if the business hits rough waters. That's why it's important to understand **when to take on debt** and **when to avoid it**.

Manu: There are certain situations where taking on debt makes sense. Here's when **TechZone** should consider borrowing:

1. Clear Growth Opportunities:

If you have a **clear, defined plan** for how the borrowed money will generate more revenue, debt can help. For example, if you know that expanding into a new market will increase sales by 30%, and you need funds to set up a new store, that's a good reason to take on debt.

2. Steady Cash Flow:

If **TechZone** has a **steady**, **predictable cash flow**, you can be confident in your ability to make the loan repayments on time. This is especially important if the loan has fixed monthly payments. If your cash flow can cover the debt payments without disrupting your other operations, borrowing could be a safe bet.

3. Low Interest Rates:

If interest rates are low, debt becomes a cheaper way to finance growth. For example, if **TechZone** can secure a loan at a low interest rate, it may be more beneficial than using cash reserves, especially if keeping those reserves allows you to stay flexible for unexpected expenses.

4. Short-Term Capital Needs:

If you have short-term capital needs, like buying inventory ahead of a big sales season or upgrading equipment to meet increasing demand, short-term loans or lines of credit can help bridge the gap without long-term debt commitments.

Vinu: So, as long as I have a clear plan, steady cash flow, and the terms are favorable, it makes sense to borrow for growth?

Manu: Exactly. The key is having a **strategy** for how the debt will help you grow and ensuring that you can comfortably make the repayments.

Manu: Now, let's talk about when to **avoid** taking on debt. Here are some red flags:

- **Uncertain Cash Flow:** If TechZone has unpredictable or seasonal cash flow, it's risky to take on debt because you might struggle to make repayments during slow months. For example, if your sales fluctuate widely, a large debt payment could strain your business during lean times.

- **No Clear Use for the Loan:** If you don't have a clear, specific use for the loan that will generate revenue, it's best to avoid borrowing. Don't take out a loan just because money is available—without a concrete plan, debt can quickly become a burden.

- **High Interest Rates or Unfavorable Terms:** If the interest rates are high or the repayment terms are unfavorable (e.g., large balloon payments), you could end up paying much more than you borrowed, which could put pressure on TechZone's finances.

- **Using Debt to Cover Losses:** If you're thinking of using debt to cover ongoing losses or operational shortfalls, stop! Debt should not be used to prop up a failing business. In this case, it's better to focus on fixing your business model before adding more financial pressure with debt.

Vinu: So, if I'm not sure how I'll use the loan, or if **TechZone** is already facing financial challenges, it's better to avoid debt?

Manu: Exactly. Debt isn't a solution for fixing fundamental problems—it's a tool for **growth** when used correctly. Now, let's talk about what to do if debt becomes unmanageable.

Vinu: What happens if I take on debt and then it starts becoming unmanageable? What should I do if **TechZone** struggles to make repayments?

Manu: If debt becomes unmanageable, don't panic. There are several steps you can take to regain control:

1. Renegotiate Terms with Lenders:

Your first step should be to contact your lender and see if you can **renegotiate the terms** of the loan. You might be able to extend the repayment period or get a lower interest rate, which would reduce your monthly payments. Lenders often prefer renegotiating to ensure they get their money back rather than seeing you default.

2. Cut Non-Essential Expenses:

Look at your expenses and identify areas where you can **cut costs**. If **TechZone** is spending on things that aren't critical to the business, like excessive marketing or unnecessary travel, cut those costs to free up cash for loan repayments.

3. Consolidate Debt:

If you have multiple loans, you might consider **consolidating** them into one loan with a lower interest rate or better terms. This simplifies your payments and might reduce the overall amount you owe monthly.

4. Increase Revenue:

Focus on ways to **boost sales** quickly. For **TechZone**, this might mean running promotions, offering discounts to drive immediate sales, or launching new products that can generate quick revenue to cover the loan payments.

5. Seek Professional Help:

If you're feeling overwhelmed, consider hiring a **financial advisor** or a **debt counselor** who can help you create a plan to manage the debt. They can offer strategies to get back on track and provide insights on how to prioritize your payments.

Vinu: That's reassuring to know. So, renegotiating terms, cutting costs, and increasing revenue can help if the debt becomes too much?

Manu: Exactly! The key is to take action early and communicate with your lender. Most lenders will work with you if they see you're serious about paying back the debt.

Vinu: What if the debt really starts weighing down **TechZone**? How do I get out of it and make sure I don't fall into the debt trap again?

Manu: Getting out of debt takes focus and discipline, but it's definitely doable. Here are the steps you can take:

1. Create a Repayment Plan:

First, sit down and create a **debt repayment plan**. List all your debts, their interest rates, and repayment terms. Prioritize paying off the loans with the highest interest rates first, as they cost you the most over time. For **TechZone**, this might mean focusing on paying off a high-interest business loan before tackling a lower-interest one.

2. Focus on Cash Flow Management:

Improve your **cash flow management** to ensure you always have enough money on hand to cover debt payments. This might involve speeding up collections, negotiating better payment terms with suppliers, or cutting unnecessary expenses.

3. Increase Profit Margins:

Look for ways to increase your **profit margins**. This could mean raising prices slightly, cutting production costs, or finding ways to reduce overhead. Every bit of extra profit can go toward paying off the debt faster.

4. Avoid Taking on New Debt:

While you're working on paying off the debt, avoid taking on new debt unless it's absolutely necessary for survival. Focus on reducing the existing debt before considering any new loans.

5. Build a Cash Reserve:

Once you're out of debt, work on building a **cash reserve**. This safety net can help you avoid relying on debt in the future if unexpected expenses arise or if there's a downturn in sales.

Vinu: That makes sense. So, by creating a repayment plan, managing cash flow better, and focusing on profitability, I can work my way out of debt. And building a cash reserve will help me avoid falling into the same trap again?

Manu: Exactly! The goal is not just to get out of debt but to set up **TechZone** so that you don't need to rely on debt in the future unless it's part of a well-thought-out growth plan.

5.2 Cost of Capital Optimization

Vinu: Manu, I've been thinking about how to make the best use of the funds I raise for **TechZone**—whether through debt or equity—but I keep hearing about something called the **cost of capital**. How does it fit into the bigger picture? I want to understand how optimizing this can help with setting goals, fixing returns, and even pricing.

Manu: Ah, you're diving into a really important concept, Vinu! **Cost of capital** is like the baseline for all your financial decisions—it's the rate of return you need to generate to justify the money you're raising, whether through debt or equity. Optimizing it can have a huge impact on your **return on investment (ROI)** targets, **overall business goals**, and even how you price your products.

Think of it this way: by lowering your cost of capital, you're reducing the overall financial burden on the business. The **lower your cost of capital**, the more flexibility you have in making decisions that boost profitability and growth.

Manu: The **cost of capital** represents the **weighted average** of what it costs you to raise funds, whether through **debt** or **equity**. Here's a breakdown:

1. Cost of Debt:

This is the interest you pay on loans or other forms of borrowing. For example, if **TechZone** takes out a loan with a 10% interest rate, that's your **cost of debt**.

2. Cost of Equity:

This is the return you need to provide to investors in exchange for their equity investment. Unlike debt, you don't have to pay interest, but equity investors expect a return in the form of **dividends** or **increased share value**. For example, if you bring on an investor who expects a 15% return, that's your **cost of equity**.

The formula for calculating the **Weighted Average Cost of Capital (WACC)** is:

WACC = (Cost of Debt × Debt / Debt + Equity)+(Cost of Equity × Equity / Debt + Equity)

By balancing these two sources of financing in the right way, you can lower your overall cost of capital, giving **TechZone** a financial edge.

Let's create a sample **Weighted Average Cost of Capital (WACC)** calculation for **TechZone**. This will illustrate how to calculate the WACC based on the proportions and costs of debt and equity financing.

Assumptions for TechZone's WACC Calculation

Debt: ₹4,00,000

Equity: ₹6,00,000

Total Capital: ₹10,00,000

Cost of Debt: 10%

Cost of Equity: 15%

Tax Rate: 30% (Since interest on debt is tax-deductible, we'll adjust the cost of debt accordingly.)

WACC Calculation for TechZone

Component	Amount (₹)	Proportion of Capital	Cost	After Tax Cost	Weighted Cost
Debt	4,00,000	4,00,000/10,00,000 = 0.4 (40%)	10%	10% x (1-0.3) = 7%	7% x 0.4 = 2.8%
Equity	6,00,000	6,00,000/10,00,000 = 0.6 (60%)	15%	N/A	15% x 0.6 = 9.0%
Total WACC	10,00,000	100%			11.8%

Manu: Vinu, let's break down this WACC calculation for TechZone so you can see how each component fits together and why it's important.

1. Debt Calculation:

We start with the debt component. TechZone's debt is ₹4,00,000, which is 40% of your total capital of ₹10,00,000. Now, since the cost of debt is 10%, you might think that's what we're working with. However, because interest is tax-deductible, we adjust this cost to reflect the after-tax rate. So, we multiply it by (1 - the tax rate), which is 30% in this case. That gives us:

$$10\% \times (1 - 0.3) = 7\%$$

Now, we multiply this after-tax cost of 7% by the 40% proportion of debt in your capital structure:

$$7\% \times 0.4 = 2.8\%$$

So, for the debt component, you're contributing 2.8% to the overall cost of capital.

2. Equity Calculation:

Next, let's look at equity. TechZone's equity stands at ₹6,00,000, which is 60% of your total capital. The cost of equity is 15%, as investors expect a return on their investment. There's no tax adjustment here since equity doesn't offer a tax shield like debt.

$$15\% \times 0.6 = 9.0\%$$

So, the equity component adds 9.0% to the overall cost of capital.

3. Total WACC:

To get your WACC, we simply add the weighted costs from both debt and equity:

$$2.8\% + 9.0\% = 11.8\%$$

Vinu: So, 11.8% is the minimum return I need to generate on any investments or projects for **TechZone** to cover the cost of raising this capital?

Manu: Exactly, Vinu! This 11.8% WACC becomes your benchmark. If you're considering an investment, it needs to deliver a return higher than 11.8% to ensure it's adding value. The lower you can keep this WACC, the less financial pressure there is on **TechZone**, giving you more room to make decisions that enhance profitability and growth.

Vinu: So, my **cost of capital** is basically the average cost of all the money I'm using to run **TechZone**, and the goal is to keep it as low as possible?

Manu: Exactly. Now, let's connect the dots between **cost of capital** and your **ROI** targets. Your **cost of capital** sets the **minimum return** you need to generate on your investments to break even.

Your **WACC** is 11.8%, then any investment you make—whether in new products, expansion, or marketing—must generate at least a 11.8% return to justify the cost of raising that capital.

1. Setting ROI Targets:

You can use your **cost of capital** as the benchmark for setting ROI targets. If you know it costs **TechZone** 11.8% to raise money, you'll want to aim for projects or investments that generate returns **higher than 11.8%.** Anything lower than that wouldn't be worth the effort, as it wouldn't even cover your cost of capital.

2. Optimizing Investments:

Let's say **TechZone** is considering investing in new technology that will cost ₹10,00,000. If your **WACC** is 15%, then you need to ensure that the return on this investment is higher than 15%—otherwise, the investment wouldn't generate enough profit to cover your capital costs.

3. Prioritizing Projects:

By understanding your **cost of capital**, you can prioritize projects that are likely to generate higher returns. For instance, if you have two projects—one with a 15% ROI and another with an 8% ROI—you'd prioritize the one with the 15% return because it exceeds your cost of capital, whereas the other would fall short.

Vinu: That makes sense. So, my **cost of capital** is like a filter that tells me what investments are worth pursuing based on whether they can generate returns higher than the cost of raising the money?

Manu: Exactly! It ensures you're not just investing for the sake of growth but making sure that growth is **profitable**. Now, let's look at how this impacts your overall business targets.

Manu: Your **cost of capital** also plays a crucial role in setting the **overall financial goals** for **TechZone**. Here's how:

1. Profitability Targets:

As we discussed, your **cost of capital** sets the **minimum return** you need to stay profitable. So, when you're setting financial targets for the year, whether it's net profit or revenue growth, you need to factor in your cost of capital. For example, if your WACC is 12%, your profit targets need to exceed this to generate real value for the business.

2. Growth Strategies:

Your growth strategies—like opening new locations, hiring more staff, or launching new products—should all be measured against your **cost of capital.** If **TechZone** is planning to expand, you need to ensure that the additional revenue will generate returns greater than your cost of capital, or you risk growing without improving profitability.

3. Long-Term Sustainability:

Managing your **cost of capital** effectively helps ensure **long-term sustainability**. If your cost of capital is too high, it will limit your ability to invest in future growth, as every rupee raised will need to generate a high return just to cover its cost. Keeping your cost of capital optimized means you can make long-term plans with less financial stress.

Vinu: So, it's not just about immediate returns—it's also about making sure the business can sustain itself and grow over the long term?

Manu: Exactly. Keeping your cost of capital low gives you more room to grow and stay profitable in the long run.

Vinu: I get how cost of capital affects investment decisions and overall targets, but how does it impact pricing strategy? Does it have a role in setting the prices of my products?

Manu: Absolutely, Vinu! Your **cost of capital** influences how you should price your products to ensure that you're generating enough profit to cover not just your direct costs but also the cost of raising capital. Here's how it works:

1. Covering Total Costs:

When you're setting prices, you need to ensure that they cover not just your **variable costs** (like production and shipping) but also your **fixed costs** (like rent and salaries) and your **cost of capital**. If your cost of capital is 10%, your prices need to be high enough to ensure that you're generating enough profit that will contribute to 10% cost of capital.

2. Determining Profit Margins:

Your **profit margins** should reflect your cost of capital. For example, if your cost of capital is high, you'll need higher profit margins to make your business viable. If **TechZone** is selling gadgets with a slim profit margin that doesn't account for the cost of capital, you might be generating revenue but still not making enough to cover the real cost of financing the business.

3. Competitive Pricing:

Understanding your **cost of capital** also helps you balance competitive pricing with profitability. If your cost of capital is high, you might have less room to lower prices in a competitive market without sacrificing profitability. However, if you manage to lower your cost of capital by optimizing your mix of debt and equity, you can afford to offer more competitive pricing without hurting your bottom line.

Vinu: So, when setting prices, I need to ensure that I'm not just covering costs but also generating enough to cover the cost of the funds I've raised?

Manu: Exactly. Without considering your **cost of capital**, you could price too low and hurt your profitability, even if your sales are strong. Now, let's talk about how to optimize the mix of debt and equity to keep your cost of capital as low as possible.

Manu: Optimizing your **cost of capital** means finding the right balance between **debt** and **equity**. Here's how you can do that:

1. Use Debt Wisely:

Debt can be cheaper than equity because interest payments on loans are tax-deductible, which lowers your **effective cost of debt**. However, too much debt increases risk, especially if your cash flow becomes tight. The goal is to take on enough debt to keep your cost of capital low, but not so much that it threatens the business's stability. For **TechZone**, this means borrowing strategically, only when you know you can make timely repayments.

2. Limit Expensive Equity:

Equity can be more expensive than debt because investors expect higher returns. While equity financing doesn't require regular payments like debt, it dilutes your ownership and usually costs more in the long run because investors expect a portion of the profits. For **TechZone**, you might want to limit equity financing to strategic investments that provide long-term benefits, like bringing on a partner with industry expertise.

3. Balance the Two:

The sweet spot is to **balance debt and equity** so that your overall cost of capital remains low. If debt becomes too risky due to high interest rates or uncertain cash flow, using equity may be a better option, and vice versa. The key is to regularly review your financial structure to ensure that you're keeping the cost of capital optimized.

Vinu: So, it's all about balance—using debt when it's cheaper and less risky, and limiting equity to avoid giving away too much control and paying high long-term costs?

Manu: Exactly! Optimizing your **cost of capital** isn't just about cutting costs—it's about making smart decisions on how you finance the business to keep your financial burden low and your profitability high.

5.3 How Paying More Tax Can Reduce Interest Costs

Vinu: Manu, I was looking at our tax payments, and it feels like a significant portion of our profits go toward taxes. I know taxes are a part of doing business, but sometimes I wonder if we could save more by cutting down on them. Does paying more tax really make a difference?

Manu: I get where you're coming from, Vinu. Paying taxes isn't exactly the most enjoyable part of running a business. However, there's actually an upside to paying the right amount of tax on time. In some cases, it can even reduce the interest costs on any financing you take on, and it strengthens your creditworthiness.

Vinu: That sounds a bit counterintuitive. How does paying more tax help us save on interest?

Manu: It's true that it sounds unusual, but here's how it works. When TechZone consistently pays its taxes on time and maintains full compliance, it reflects positively on your business's financial health. Lenders look at tax compliance as a sign of stability, which can lead to lower interest rates on loans or credit lines.

1. Strengthening Financial Credibility

Manu: Lenders view tax compliance as a good indicator of financial stability. When you're regularly paying taxes and reporting accurate profits, it shows that TechZone is financially healthy and responsibly managed. This helps lenders feel more confident in your business, which can translate into lower interest rates.

Vinu: So, lenders are more willing to offer better terms if they see that we're keeping up with taxes?

Manu: Exactly. When lenders see consistent tax payments, they view TechZone as a lower-risk borrower. They're more likely to offer you better interest rates because they trust that you have stable income and are managing your finances well. Lower interest rates mean lower overall costs for the loan.

2. Impact on Loan Approval

Vinu: I see. But what happens if we were to under-report income to save on taxes? Would that affect us when we're applying for a loan?

Manu: Yes, under-reporting income can actually hurt your chances of getting favorable loan terms—or even getting approved at all. When you show lower profits on your tax returns, lenders might assume TechZone is less profitable than it actually is, which can lead them to either charge higher interest rates or deny the loan.

Vinu: So, by reporting accurate income, even if it means paying more tax, we're showing lenders that we're financially strong?

Manu: That's right. When you pay taxes on accurate income, you're demonstrating healthy profit margins. This shows lenders that TechZone is stable and capable of repaying loans. It's about building credibility and showing that your business is financially secure, which ultimately works in your favor.

3. Avoiding Tax Penalties and Interest

Vinu: What about tax penalties? Do they really make that much of a difference?

Manu: They can make a huge difference. If taxes are underpaid or unpaid, you could incur penalties and interest from tax authorities. These extra charges can add up quickly and, in some cases, cost more than what you would have saved by under-reporting income.

Vinu: So, by paying the right amount of tax upfront, we avoid those penalties and the interest that could come with them?

Manu: Exactly. Consistently paying the correct amount ensures that TechZone avoids these unnecessary costs. It keeps you out of trouble with tax authorities, and you avoid any surprise charges that could affect cash flow. Plus, it keeps your financial statements accurate, which is important for lenders to see.

4. Access to Better Financing Options

Vinu: Okay, that makes sense. Are there other advantages when it comes to financing?

Manu: Yes! By maintaining full tax compliance, you position TechZone as a reliable and responsible business. Banks and investors appreciate that, and they may be more willing to offer better financing options. When lenders see that TechZone is paying taxes on time and showing consistent profits, they're more likely to offer favorable loan terms, including lower interest rates.

Vinu: So, better compliance can actually give us an edge when it comes to borrowing?

Manu: Absolutely. Being a responsible taxpayer can make your business more attractive to lenders. They'll see you as a lower-risk borrower, which increases your chances of getting lower interest rates and better terms. It's a strategic way to improve your financial options without even negotiating— it's all in your track record.

Final Thoughts on Tax Compliance and Interest Costs

Vinu: I hadn't realized that paying taxes could impact our financing so much. It sounds like, by staying compliant and showing solid profits, we're actually saving money in the long run, even if we're paying a bit more in tax.

Manu: Exactly, Vinu. It's a long-term strategy. By building a strong financial profile through tax compliance, you're not only avoiding penalties but also creating opportunities for better financing. So yes, paying the right amount of tax might seem like a higher cost upfront, but it can actually help you save on interest and give you access to better financial resources.

Vinu: Thanks, Manu. This helps me see tax payments in a new light—less as a burden and more as an investment in TechZone's financial reputation.

Manu: That's the right perspective! By being proactive and responsible with taxes, you're positioning TechZone as a strong, reliable business. In the end, it helps you grow with better financing options and a lower overall cost of capital.

5.4 Understanding Different Types of Business Loans

Manu: Vinu, as your business grows, there may be times when you need external financing to support expansion, cover working capital needs, or manage cash flow. Different types of loans and credit products are designed for various purposes, and understanding each one can help you make smart financial choices.

Vinu: That's definitely something I want to know more about. I've heard terms like cash credit, letter of credit, and term loan, but I'm not sure when to use them or how they differ.

Manu: No problem! Let's walk through some of the most common types of credit products. We'll cover what they are, when they're useful, and a few mistakes to avoid with each one.

1. Cash Credit (CC)

Manu: Let's start with **Cash Credit (CC)**. Cash credit is a type of short-term loan that helps cover day-to-day working capital needs. With a CC, the bank allows you to withdraw funds up to a certain limit based on your inventory or receivables. You only pay interest on the amount you actually use.

Vinu: So, it's like having an overdraft on a personal account but for business purposes?

Manu: Exactly! Cash credit is useful when you have fluctuating cash flow or need a buffer to handle operational expenses. For example, if you need to buy inventory before your sales come in, CC can bridge that gap.

Vinu: When would be the best time to use cash credit?

Manu: It's best to use cash credit for short-term needs, like buying raw materials, covering payroll, or other operational expenses. Avoid using it for long-term investments because it's a short-term product. You want to repay it as quickly as possible to minimize interest costs.

Vinu: Are there any common mistakes businesses make with cash credit?

Manu: Yes, a big mistake is relying too heavily on cash credit and keeping the account overdrawn for extended periods. This can lead to high interest expenses and dependency on short-term borrowing. Always ensure you're using cash credit for temporary cash flow needs, not ongoing expenses.

2. Letter of Credit (LC)

Manu: Next, let's talk about a **Letter of Credit (LC)**. A letter of credit is a financial guarantee from your bank that assures your supplier they will be paid. It's commonly used in international trade. For instance, if you're importing goods from overseas, your bank issues an LC to the supplier's bank, promising payment once the supplier meets the terms of the contract, like shipping the goods.

Vinu: So it's essentially a guarantee of payment to the supplier?

Manu: Yes, it gives the supplier confidence that they'll get paid. An LC is beneficial for both parties: the supplier knows they'll receive payment, and you know the payment will only go through once the agreed-upon terms are met.

Vinu: When should I consider using an LC?

Manu: Use an LC when you're dealing with new suppliers, especially in international trade, where there's a higher risk of delays or misunderstandings. It's a way to build trust with suppliers, particularly when you haven't established a long-standing relationship with them.

Vinu: What mistakes should I avoid with a letter of credit?

Manu: One mistake is not being specific about the terms. If the terms of the LC are too broad or unclear, there can be disputes about whether the conditions were met. Also, since banks charge fees for LCs, make sure the transaction is worth the cost of setting up the LC.

3. Bank Guarantee

Manu: A **Bank Guarantee** is another useful tool, especially for large projects or contracts. It's a promise from the bank that if you fail to meet your obligations—like completing a project or delivering products—the bank will pay the other party on your behalf. There are two types: financial guarantees and performance guarantees.

Vinu: So, if I'm bidding for a big contract, a bank guarantee might help me win the bid?

Manu: Absolutely. It provides assurance to the client or partner that even if something goes wrong, they won't lose their money. Bank guarantees are commonly used in construction, services, and other industries where large contracts are awarded.

Vinu: Is there a specific time when a bank guarantee is most useful?

Manu: A bank guarantee is ideal when entering into significant contracts or agreements that require a commitment to performance or payment. If the client or partner requires financial backing, a bank guarantee shows you're serious and financially stable enough to take on the project.

Vinu: Are there any potential pitfalls?

Manu: One mistake is over-committing to too many guarantees. Each bank guarantee ties up your credit capacity, so if you take on too many, it can limit your ability to secure other forms of financing. Also, if you fail to meet the obligations, the bank will pay, but they'll seek reimbursement from you, so you must be confident you can fulfill the commitment.

4. Term Loan

Manu: Now let's look at a **Term Loan**. A term loan is a loan you take out for a specific period to fund long-term investments. It could be for buying equipment, expanding operations, or even purchasing property. The loan is repaid in regular installments over a set term, often with a fixed interest rate.

Vinu: So, term loans are better for big investments rather than day-to-day expenses?

Manu: Exactly. Term loans are designed for long-term projects that will provide a return over time. For instance, if you're opening a new branch or buying machinery that will last for years, a term loan spreads the cost over the lifespan of the investment.

Vinu: When should I consider taking out a term loan?

Manu: You should consider a term loan when you're planning a project that will generate revenue over time. If the investment will improve productivity or increase sales, a term loan can help you achieve those goals without tying up all your cash.

Vinu: What mistakes should I watch out for with term loans?

Manu: Avoid taking on a term loan without a clear repayment plan. Since term loans are a longer commitment, it's important to make sure the expected returns from the investment will cover the loan payments. Also, avoid using a term loan for short-term needs, as you'll be stuck repaying it long after the benefit has been realized.

5. Export Credit

Manu: Finally, there's **Export Credit**. Export credit is a specialized type of financing for businesses that export goods or services. It helps cover the costs involved in producing and shipping goods before the payment from the buyer is received. Export credit comes in various forms, such as pre-shipment and post-shipment finance.

Vinu: How does export credit work, and when would I need it?

Manu: Let's say you have an order from a foreign buyer but need funds to produce and ship the goods. Export credit provides that working capital so you can fulfill the order. Pre-shipment credit covers the cost of production, while post-shipment credit provides funds based on the export invoices, allowing you to get paid immediately after shipping.

Vinu: What are the main benefits of export credit?

Manu: Export credit helps you maintain smooth cash flow and reduces the financial strain of waiting for payment from overseas buyers. It also lets you offer competitive terms to customers, which can give you an edge in the international market.

Vinu: And what mistakes should I avoid with export credit?

Manu: The main pitfall is not matching the type of credit to your cash flow needs. If you take on too much export credit and the buyer delays payment, you could be stuck with a debt you can't cover. Make sure you're working with reliable buyers and that you have proper insurance in place if needed.

Manu: Each of these credit products serves a specific purpose, so it's important to match the right one to the right need. Cash credit helps with working capital, letters of credit and bank guarantees support transactions and commitments, term loans fund long-term investments, and export credit facilitates international trade.

Vinu: It sounds like a lot to keep track of, but it really makes sense to use the right tool for each financial need. And I'll definitely keep an eye out for the mistakes you mentioned.

Manu: That's the key, Vinu. With the right understanding, these tools can help your business grow and run smoothly. But if you use them incorrectly or become over-reliant, they can create financial strain.

Vinu: Thanks, Manu. I feel like I have a much better understanding and I'm ready to learn more.

5.5 Managing Bank Loans for Better Profitability and Financial Health

Smart Loan Management for Profitability

Vinu: Manu, we've talked about choosing the right type of credit product, but I'm looking for ways to manage loans more efficiently. I want to make sure TechZone isn't spending more on loans than we have to. Can you walk me through the different charges we need to watch out for and how we can minimize them?

Manu: Absolutely, Vinu. Managing a loan effectively isn't just about keeping up with the EMIs—it's about understanding the full scope of charges and fees that come with it. These charges can add up quickly, impacting your cash flow and profitability. By learning about these costs, you'll know where to cut back, negotiate, and avoid unnecessary fees. Let's go over some of the common charges and strategies for managing them.

1. Interest Rates: Fixed and Floating

Vinu: Let's start with interest rates. I understand there are both fixed and floating rates, but which one is best for keeping costs low?

Manu: Great question. Here's how they work:

- **Fixed Interest Rates** stay constant over the loan term, giving you predictable payments, which is ideal if you expect rates to rise. They're a good option if TechZone has stable cash flow and you want consistency.

- **Floating Interest Rates** fluctuate based on market conditions, which can mean lower initial payments, but there's a risk of rates going up. They're usually a better choice when rates are low or expected to fall, as they can reduce costs over time.

For TechZone, consider your cash flow and risk tolerance. If you want predictability, fixed rates work best. If you're comfortable with variability, floating rates could save you money.

2. Processing, Upfront, and Loan Cancellation Charges

Vinu: I've noticed banks charge processing fees and sometimes upfront charges at disbursal. Are these negotiable?

Manu: Yes, many banks are willing to negotiate these fees, especially if you're a repeat customer or have a solid financial track record. Here's a breakdown:

- **Processing Fees**: These are one-time fees for processing the loan application. Ask if the bank can reduce them, especially for larger loans or repeat business.

- **Upfront Charges**: These are fees charged when the loan is disbursed. Similar to processing fees, you may be able to negotiate a reduction or waiver.

- **Loan Cancellation Fees**: If you decide to cancel a loan after approval but before disbursement, banks may charge a cancellation fee. To avoid this, make sure you're certain about your financing needs before finalizing any loan agreements.

Vinu: So, negotiation is key here. It sounds like banks can be flexible if they see you're serious about maintaining a good relationship.

Manu: Absolutely. Don't hesitate to ask for reductions, especially if you're bringing regular business or have an excellent credit history. Reducing these upfront costs is a smart way to lower your overall borrowing expenses.

3. Prepayment, Foreclosure, and Repricing Fees

Vinu: What if I want to pay off the loan early? Are there charges for prepayment or foreclosure?

Manu: Yes, some banks do charge for early repayments:

- **Prepayment Fees**: These apply if you pay off part of your loan early. Fixed-rate loans often come with higher prepayment charges, so it's something to watch for if you're planning on paying down the loan ahead of schedule.

- **Foreclosure Charges**: These fees apply if you pay off the entire loan before the term ends. Many banks offer a partial or full waiver on these fees, especially if you've been a reliable customer.

- **Repricing Fees**: If you're on a fixed rate and want to switch to floating (or vice versa), some banks charge a repricing fee. This can be worth it if market rates drop significantly and you want to take advantage of a lower rate.

Vinu: Is it generally worth paying these fees to reduce the loan balance early?

Manu: If you have excess cash flow and the fees are manageable, prepaying can save you on interest costs in the long run. Always compare the prepayment fee with the interest savings before deciding.

4. Overdue Interest, Penal Interest, and Bounce Charges

Vinu: I understand the basics of overdue and penal interest, but how do I make sure TechZone doesn't get hit with these charges?

Manu: Staying on top of payments is crucial to avoid these extra costs. Here's how each charge works:

- **Overdue Interest**: Charged when you miss a payment, often at a higher rate than the standard interest. Avoid this by setting up automated payments or reminders.

- **Penal Interest**: This fee is for non-compliance with loan terms, like not maintaining certain account balances. Make sure to review your loan agreement and comply with all conditions.

- **Bounce Charges**: When a payment or cheque bounces due to insufficient funds, banks charge a fee. Avoid these by ensuring the account linked to your loan has sufficient funds.

Vinu: So, it's all about staying organized and keeping communication open with the bank?

Manu: Exactly. Regularly review your loan terms and payment schedules, and if you anticipate any payment issues, reach out to the bank proactively. It can save you from unnecessary costs and maintain your credibility.

5. Commitment Charges and Account Maintenance Fees

Vinu: What about **commitment charges** for cash credit lines and **account maintenance fees**? Are these avoidable?

Manu: To some extent, yes. Here's how they work:

- **Commitment Charges**: If you have a cash credit or overdraft facility, banks charge for unused limits if you don't utilize the funds. To minimize this, plan to draw only as much credit as you need. If TechZone often has unused limits, consider reducing the facility amount.

- **Account Maintenance Fees**: These are periodic fees for maintaining the account associated with your loan. Some banks waive them if you maintain a minimum balance, so review the account terms and keep balances at the required level.

Vinu: So, I should draw only what we need and make sure our balances meet minimum requirements to avoid these fees?

Manu: Exactly. It's about matching your credit facility to your actual cash needs and monitoring account balances. Small adjustments here can reduce unnecessary costs.

6. Other Potential Fees: Stamp Duty, Legal, and Technical Valuation Charges

Vinu: I've noticed some fees that are not directly loan-related, like **stamp duty** and **legal charges**. Can you explain these?

Manu: Of course. These fees often come with secured loans:

- **Stamp Duty**: Required for legalizing loan documents, and rates vary by state. It's typically unavoidable, so just plan for it as part of the loan setup cost.

- **Legal Charges**: If the bank needs to verify collateral, like property, they may charge for legal services. Confirm if the bank has a preferred panel of lawyers, as this can reduce costs.

- **Technical Valuation Fees**: For secured loans, banks may conduct technical evaluations of the collateral, such as property appraisals. You can sometimes negotiate a reduction here, especially if you're using collateral the bank has valued recently.

Vinu: So, while some fees are mandatory, there's often room to negotiate or reduce them by understanding the bank's processes?

Manu: Precisely. Knowing what's mandatory versus negotiable can save you money. Always ask for a fee breakdown and see where there's room for adjustment.

7. Maintaining Good Credit to Reduce Borrowing Costs

Vinu: Beyond managing these individual charges, how can I maintain TechZone's credibility with the bank?

Manu: Here are some tips for building and maintaining strong creditworthiness:

- **Regular On-Time Payments**: This is fundamental. Paying EMIs on time demonstrates reliability, which can lead to better terms for future loans.

- **Transparency and Communication**: Keep an open line with your bank about TechZone's financial health. If there's ever a risk of missing a payment, communicate in advance. Banks appreciate proactive borrowers.

- **Periodic Loan Reviews**: Schedule reviews with your bank, especially if TechZone's credit improves or market rates change. You may be able to renegotiate terms or secure a lower rate.

Vinu: It sounds like maintaining a solid relationship with the bank is essential, and it can also open doors for better terms down the line.

Manu: Absolutely. Banks value consistency, transparency, and strong financial management. Over time, this relationship can help you negotiate lower rates, avoid certain charges, and access more favorable financing.

8. Building a Comprehensive Loan Management Strategy

Vinu: So, how do I bring all this together to create a strategy for TechZone that optimizes loan management and reduces costs?

Manu: Let's summarize a holistic approach:

- **Negotiate Upfront Costs**: Work with the bank to reduce processing, upfront, and legal fees. Also, clarify any prepayment and foreclosure charges so you can plan around them.

- **Optimize Cash Flow**: Use credit facilities wisely to avoid commitment charges. For example, draw cash credit as needed, and align cash inflows with loan repayments to prevent bounce charges.

- **Monitor Terms and Conditions**: Ensure compliance with all loan terms to avoid penal interest. Review the facility annually to adjust limits or terms if needed.

- **Leverage Banking Relationships**: Cultivate strong bank relationships by being proactive and transparent. This can lead to better negotiation power for future loans.

Vinu: Thanks, Manu! With these strategies, I feel more prepared to make informed decisions about managing TechZone's loans and reducing costs.

Manu: You're welcome, Vinu. Effective loan management not only lowers costs but also positions TechZone for sustainable growth and stronger profitability.

Chapter 6 - Asset and Resource Management

6.1 Asset Management

Vinu: Manu, I've been thinking about how **TechZone** can better utilize its assets for growth, but I'm not sure how to approach it. I want to make sure that the assets we invest in actually help the business grow. Could you walk me through how I should be thinking about **asset management?**

Manu: Absolutely, Vinu! **Asset management** is a crucial part of running a business successfully because it's not just about buying assets—it's about ensuring those assets are **working hard** for your business. Whether we're talking about **tangible assets** like equipment and machinery, or **intangible assets** like intellectual property or brand reputation, they all need to be **properly managed** to contribute to your business goals.

Let's break down how you can leverage asset management to drive growth at **TechZone** and avoid unnecessary burdens.

Manu: First, think of assets as the tools that help you reach your business goals. Every asset you acquire—whether it's a machine, a software system, or a patent—should have a clear purpose that aligns with your long-term objectives. Here's how to think about it:

1. Goal Alignment:

Before purchasing any asset, ask yourself: **How will this asset help me achieve my business goals?** For example, if **TechZone** is aiming to increase production capacity, buying new equipment that allows you to produce more gadgets faster would align with that goal.

2. Revenue-Generating vs. Supportive Assets:

Focus on acquiring **revenue-generating assets** first. These are assets that directly contribute to your ability to make more money. For **TechZone**, this might be high-performance manufacturing equipment that allows you to produce gadgets more efficiently and meet market demand.

Supportive assets—like administrative software—are also important, but they should come second to assets that help you **generate revenue** or **reduce costs**. For example, an advanced customer relationship management (CRM) system might not directly generate revenue, but it helps streamline sales processes and improve customer service, ultimately leading to higher sales.

Vinu: So, the key is to focus on assets that either **generate revenue** or **support** the generation of revenue, rather than just buying something because it seems useful?

Manu: Exactly! Each asset should be part of a broader **strategic plan**—it's either helping you make more money or making your operations more efficient. Now, let's talk about the kinds of assets you should focus on and which ones to avoid.

Manu: When it comes to acquiring assets, your focus should be on those that either **drive revenue** or **reduce costs**. Here's what to look for:

1. Revenue-Generating Assets:

These are assets that directly contribute to your ability to grow sales or expand your market. For **TechZone**, this could mean:

- **Manufacturing equipment** that increases production capacity.

- **Technology upgrades** that enable you to deliver new products faster or improve product quality.

- **Distribution channels,** such as delivery vehicles, that help you get products to customers more efficiently.

2. Cost-Reducing Assets:

Another valuable type of asset is one that helps you reduce your operating costs. For example:

- **Automation tools:** If you invest in software or machinery that automates repetitive tasks, you reduce labor costs and minimize errors.

- **Energy-efficient equipment:** Switching to energy-efficient lighting, appliances, or manufacturing tools can cut your utility bills over time.

In both cases, the goal is to invest in assets that either **improve your bottom line** by generating more revenue or **reduce expenses**, making your business more profitable in the long run.

Vinu: That makes sense. So, I should prioritize assets **that either make me more money** or **save me money** by reducing costs. But what about assets that don't fit into these categories?

Manu: Exactly. You should avoid purchasing **assets that don't contribute** to your business goals, especially those that become **financial burdens.** Here's what to stay away from:

1. Non-Essential Assets:

Avoid purchasing assets that are more of a **luxury** than a necessity, especially if they don't directly contribute to your ability to generate income. For **TechZone**, this could be something like buying overly expensive office furniture or luxury company cars that don't contribute to the core operations of the business.

2. Assets with High Maintenance Costs and Low ROI:

Some assets come with **high ongoing costs** for maintenance, repairs, or upkeep but don't generate enough revenue or savings to justify those expenses. For instance, a piece of equipment that requires frequent maintenance or doesn't get used often will end up being a drain on your cash flow. In **TechZone's** case, investing in a machine that only gets used occasionally but costs a lot to maintain wouldn't be worth it.

3. Assets That Quickly Depreciate:

Be cautious of assets that **lose value rapidly** without generating significant returns. For example, vehicles tend to depreciate quickly, so unless you need them for critical business operations (like deliveries), it might not be a wise investment. Similarly, gadgets or tech tools that become obsolete quickly may not provide long-term value.

Vinu: Got it. So, I should avoid assets that are more for show than for function, and anything that will drain resources without contributing enough to revenue or cost savings?

Manu: Exactly. The focus should always be on assets that **work for your business**, not those that end up being a **burden**. Now, let's talk about how to manage the assets you already have to get the **maximum benefit** from them.

Manu: Once you've acquired the right assets, it's important to **manage** them properly to ensure they're delivering the maximum value. Here's how you can do that:

1. Regular Maintenance and Upkeep:

For tangible assets like equipment and machinery, make sure they're regularly **maintained** to keep them running efficiently. Downtime due to broken or poorly maintained equipment can cost you more in the long run. For **TechZone**, scheduling regular maintenance for your production machines will ensure they operate at full capacity, helping you meet customer demand without costly breakdowns.

2. Monitor Asset Performance:

Keep track of how well your assets are performing. For example, if you've invested in software to streamline operations, monitor whether it's actually improving efficiency or saving time. If an asset isn't providing the expected return, it might be time to consider upgrading or replacing it. In **TechZone**, if a machine that's supposed to increase productivity isn't meeting its targets, it's worth evaluating why that's happening.

3. Use Assets to Their Full Potential:

Ensure that your assets are being used to their full capacity. If you've invested in a piece of equipment that can produce 1,000 units per day but you're only using it for 500 units, you're not getting the full value out of the asset. For **TechZone**, if you're not fully utilizing the manufacturing equipment, consider taking on more orders or increasing production to make the most of your investment.

4. Asset Tracking and Depreciation Management:

Keep detailed records of your assets, including when they were purchased, their expected lifespan, and their **depreciation** schedule. This helps you plan for replacements or upgrades. For **TechZone**, knowing when a piece of equipment will likely need to be replaced means you can start budgeting early rather than facing a sudden, unexpected expense.

5. Upgrade When Necessary:

Sometimes, upgrading to a newer model or more efficient asset is the best way to get more out of your investment. If a machine or software tool is outdated and slowing down your operations, it might be time to reinvest in a newer, faster version. For **TechZone**, upgrading your production line with more advanced technology could result in higher output and lower costs.

Vinu: That's really helpful. So, I need to take care of maintenance, track performance, fully use what I've got, and upgrade when necessary to make sure my assets are giving me the best return?

Manu: Exactly! Proper **asset management** is about **optimizing** what you already have to ensure it's contributing to your business goals and **maximizing value** over time.

Vinu: That's really helpful, Manu. But how do I know if an investment in a particular asset is worthwhile? Is there a way to evaluate it before buying?

Manu: Definitely! When making investment decisions, it's crucial to use financial tools to determine if an asset will deliver a good return. **Net Present Value (NPV), Internal Rate of Return (IRR), and Discounted Cash Flow (DCF)** techniques are great for this. These tools help you assess the potential returns of an investment compared to its costs.

1. Net Present Value (NPV):

NPV helps you estimate the value an investment will bring over time, accounting for the cost of capital. For example, if **TechZone** is considering a ₹5,00,000 investment in new equipment, NPV will help you see if the future cash flows generated by that equipment will exceed its cost. A positive NPV means the investment is worthwhile.

2. Internal Rate of Return (IRR):

IRR is the rate at which an investment's future cash flows equal its initial cost. It tells you the potential profitability. If the IRR is higher than **TechZone's** cost of capital, the investment makes sense. For instance, if you're comparing multiple projects, choose the one with the highest IRR, provided it meets your strategic goals.

3. Discounted Cash Flow (DCF):

DCF calculates the present value of future cash flows from an investment. For **TechZone**, if you're evaluating a project expected to bring in ₹1,00,000 yearly, DCF helps you decide if those future earnings justify today's costs.

Vinu: These tools sound useful, but they're also a bit technical. Is there somewhere I can learn more about them?

Manu: Absolutely! There are free videos on the **CA Raja Classes YouTube channel** that cover **NPV**, **IRR**, and **DCF** techniques in detail. These videos explain how to use each tool step-by-step, so you can feel confident in evaluating investments for **TechZone**.

Manu: There are a few other key elements of **asset management** to keep in mind:

1. Asset Life cycles:

Every asset has a **lifecycle**—from acquisition to usage to disposal. Understanding this helps you plan for the long term. For example, some assets might need to be replaced every 5 years, while others might last 10 years or more. Plan for future asset replacements or upgrades so you're not caught off guard when something reaches the end of its useful life.

2. Leasing vs. Buying:

Sometimes, it makes more sense to **lease** an asset rather than buying it outright. For assets that quickly become outdated (like technology), leasing allows you to use the latest tools without a large upfront investment. For **TechZone**, leasing equipment might be an option if the technology is rapidly evolving, ensuring you always have access to the latest equipment without having to buy and sell frequently.

3. Intangible Asset Management:

Don't forget about **intangible assets** like patents, trademarks, or even your brand reputation. These assets can be just as valuable as physical equipment, especially when it comes to differentiating your products in the market. Protecting and managing these intangible assets is crucial for long-term growth.

Vinu: That's really insightful. So, it's not just about the tangible stuff like equipment, but also things like brand and intellectual property that I need to manage carefully?

Manu: Exactly. **Intangible assets** can be incredibly valuable, and managing them well ensures you're fully leveraging everything that makes **TechZone** unique and competitive in the marketplace.

6.2 Managing Inventory and Supply Chain

Vinu: Manu, I've been hearing a lot about the importance of managing inventory and the supply chain, but I feel like I'm just reacting to problems instead of being proactive. I want to make sure **TechZone** is running efficiently, but I don't really know where to start with inventory and supply chain optimization. Can you help me understand how to approach this?

Manu: Absolutely, Vinu! Managing inventory and optimizing your supply chain are essential for reducing costs, improving cash flow, and increasing overall efficiency. When you get this right, **TechZone** will operate smoothly—you'll have the right products, in the right quantity, at the right time, and avoid issues like overstocking or shortages.

Let's break it down into two areas: **inventory management** and **supply chain optimization.**

Inventory Management

Manu: Inventory management is all about balancing supply and demand. You want enough inventory to meet customer needs, but not so much that it ties up cash or risks becoming outdated.

Here's what you need to focus on:

1. Inventory Levels:

Too much inventory can lead to wasted resources and higher storage costs. On the other hand, too little means you can't fulfill orders, leading to lost sales. The goal is finding the optimal level—where you meet demand without overstocking.

For example, let's say **TechZone** sells **1,000 units** of a particular gadget each month. You might aim to keep **1.5 months' worth of inventory** on hand, or

1,500 units, to cover fluctuations in demand. This way, you have a cushion without overcommitting to excess stock.

2. Demand Forecasting:

Forecasting demand accurately helps you maintain the right inventory levels. Look at past sales data, understand seasonal trends, and keep an eye on market conditions.

Suppose **TechZone** sold **10,000 units** last quarter, with **40%** of sales happening in the last month. By forecasting demand for the upcoming months based on this trend, you can adjust your inventory orders to match likely sales patterns.

3. Just-in-Time (JIT) Inventory:

A JIT system means you're ordering stock only when you need it, rather than keeping large amounts on hand. This reduces storage costs and frees up cash.

For **TechZone**, if you need **500 units** every two weeks, you'd order **500 units** on a bi-weekly basis, rather than holding **2,000 units** for a month. This way, you're minimizing the cash tied up in inventory.

4. Inventory Turnover Ratio:

This ratio shows how quickly you're selling through your stock. A high turnover ratio means your inventory is moving quickly, while a low ratio might indicate overstocking or slow-moving items.

Let's say **TechZone** has **₹5,00,000** worth of inventory and generates **₹20,00,000** in annual sales. The inventory turnover ratio would be: Inventory Turnover Ratio = Annual Sales / Average Inventory = ₹20,00,000 / ₹5,00,000 = 4. This means you're selling through your inventory four times a year. A higher ratio is often better, indicating efficient inventory management.

Vinu: So, it's about finding the balance between having enough inventory to meet demand without tying up too much cash or letting products sit for too long. What about the supply chain side?

Supply Chain Optimization

Manu: Your supply chain is what brings products from your suppliers to **TechZone** and ultimately to your customers. Optimizing it means making it efficient, while maintaining quality and availability. Here's how:

1. Supplier Relationships:

Build strong relationships with suppliers for consistent inventory levels and reduced lead times. Good suppliers are more likely to offer better terms, like longer payment periods or discounts.

For instance, if **TechZone** orders ₹3,00,000 worth of gadgets monthly, you could negotiate with your supplier for a **5% discount** on orders above ₹2,50,000. That's an instant savings of ₹15,000 each month.

2. Lead Time Reduction:

Lead time is the time between placing an order and receiving it. Reducing lead times helps you respond to customer demand quickly, without needing as much inventory on hand.

If **TechZone** usually waits **10 days** for delivery after placing an order, you could work with your supplier to reduce this to **7 days**. This enables you to keep less inventory on hand, lowering storage costs.

3. Supply Chain Visibility:

Real-time visibility helps you track where inventory is at all times, spotting delays or bottlenecks early.

Imagine **TechZone** can track shipments through an online portal, giving you updates on whether products are on schedule. This allows you to make quick adjustments, like expediting an order if a delay is detected.

3. Risk Management:

Supply chains can be disrupted by various issues, from supplier delays to natural disasters. Identify risks and have backup plans in place.

For **TechZone**, if you rely on a single supplier for a key component, consider finding a second supplier as a backup. This way, if one supplier faces delays, you have an alternative source.

4. Technology Integration:

Using inventory management or supply chain management software can automate processes, reduce errors, and provide real-time data for better decisions.

For **TechZone**, an inventory management system can track stock levels automatically. If your sales data shows a gadget is selling quickly, the system can trigger a reorder, ensuring you never run out.

Applying These Concepts to TechZone

Manu: Now, let's apply these concepts to **TechZone**. As your business grows, managing inventory and the supply chain becomes even more critical.

1. Optimizing Inventory Levels:

If **TechZone** sells different gadgets, some might always be in demand, while others sit in storage.

For high-demand items, say you sell **200 units** weekly, aim to keep **400 units** in stock as a buffer. For slow-moving items, keep stock to a minimum—maybe only **50 units**—or consider phasing them out.

2. Implementing Just-in-Time Inventory:

If **TechZone** has high storage costs, you could implement JIT for products that have reliable, quick delivery from suppliers.

For example, if a supplier can deliver **300 units** every 5 days, you only order **300 units** at a time, which reduces cash tied up in excess stock and lowers storage expenses.

3. Improving Supplier Relationships and Lead Times:

Strong supplier relationships can improve payment terms and delivery schedules. If **TechZone** negotiates a shorter lead time, you won't need as much inventory on hand.

Say you previously held **500 units** of a fast-moving product because the supplier took **10 days** to deliver. By reducing the lead time to **7 days**, you can cut that stock level to **350 units**, freeing up cash for other investments.

4. Tracking Inventory Turnover:

Monitoring turnover helps you see how quickly each product is selling. For example, if **TechZone** has **₹2,00,000** worth of a particular gadget but only sells **₹50,000** worth each quarter, that's a low turnover.

In that case, reduce future orders for that item, focus on promoting it to increase sales, or consider replacing it with a more popular product.

5. Managing Supply Chain Risk:

Always have a backup plan. For **TechZone**, this could mean working with a second supplier for critical products, so you're not completely dependent on one source.

If a supplier usually delivers a key component in **5 days**, consider having an agreement with another supplier who can deliver in **6 or 7 days** if needed. This small adjustment ensures continuity if your primary supplier faces issues.

6. Using Technology to Streamline Operations:

As **TechZone** grows, investing in inventory management software will make tracking stock and orders easier.

With real-time visibility, you can see which products are running low and reorder automatically, ensuring you're always meeting customer demand without overstocking.

Vinu: That's really helpful! So, for **TechZone**, I need to focus on forecasting demand, using JIT where possible, and keeping a close eye on product sales. I'll also work on strengthening supplier relationships and having backup plans for disruptions.

Manu: Exactly, Vinu! By optimizing both your inventory and supply chain, you'll reduce costs, improve cash flow, and enhance efficiency. And as

TechZone grows, having a solid strategy in place will help you scale smoothly and profitably.

Chapter 7 - Risk Management and Financial Governance

7.1 Risk Management: Identify financial risks and implement strategies to mitigate them

7.2 Financial Governance and Internal Controls

7.1 Risk Management: Identify financial risks and implement strategies to mitigate them

Vinu: Manu, I know that running a business comes with a lot of risks, but I'm not entirely sure how to identify them or what steps I should take to protect **TechZone** from potential financial problems. I want to be proactive instead of waiting for something to go wrong. Can you guide me through how to approach risk management?

Manu: Absolutely, Vinu! Risk management is essential, and it's all about identifying potential risks that could negatively impact your business and then taking steps to mitigate them. For **TechZone**, risk management means understanding what could threaten your financial stability—whether it's internal, like cash flow issues, or external, like changes in the market or supply chain disruptions.

Step 1: Identify Key Risks

Manu: Let's start by identifying the various risks **TechZone** might face. Here are the main categories to consider:

1. Market Risk:

This includes changes in customer demand, competitor activity, or economic downturns. For example, if **TechZone's** gadgets suddenly face new competition, sales might drop. Let's say you currently sell ₹10,00,000 worth of gadgets monthly. If a competitor releases a similar product at a lower price, you could see a **20%** decline, which means ₹2,00,000 less in revenue.

2. Credit Risk:

This risk arises when customers fail to pay on time. Imagine **TechZone** has ₹5,00,000 in credit sales each month, with ₹1,00,000 of it consistently late by 30 days. That delay affects your cash flow and could prevent you from covering short-term expenses.

3. Liquidity Risk:

Liquidity risk is the danger of running out of cash. If **TechZone** needs ₹3,00,000 monthly to cover fixed costs, having a buffer can help. But if your monthly cash flow fluctuates between ₹2,50,000 and ₹4,00,000, you're at risk during low months.

4. Operational Risk:

This includes risks like supply chain disruptions or equipment breakdowns. If a machine failure means **TechZone** can't fulfill an order worth ₹1,50,000, that's lost revenue and potential reputation damage.

5. Interest Rate Risk:

If **TechZone** has loans with variable interest rates, you might face higher payments if rates go up. For instance, a ₹10,00,000 loan at a current rate of 10% costs ₹1,00,000 per year. If the rate increases to 12%, your annual interest jumps to ₹1,20,000, tightening cash flow.

6. Foreign Exchange Risk:

If you purchase inventory from overseas suppliers, currency fluctuations can impact costs. Say **TechZone** buys $10,000 worth of components monthly. If the exchange rate moves from ₹75 to ₹80 per dollar, the cost jumps from ₹7,50,000 to ₹8,00,000, squeezing margins.

7. Compliance Risk:

Non-compliance with regulations can lead to fines. For example, if **TechZone** fails to file taxes properly, you might face penalties costing thousands. Staying updated with industry regulations helps you avoid these risks.

Vinu: Wow, I didn't realize there were so many different types of risks. So, the first step is identifying all the potential risks that could affect **TechZone**, both internally and externally?

Manu: Exactly, Vinu. Once you've identified these risks, the next step is to implement strategies to manage them.

Step 2: Mitigating Key Risks

Manu: Now, let's look at how to mitigate each of these risks:

1. Managing Market Risk:

Diversify product offerings and monitor industry trends. If **TechZone** notices a shift toward wearable gadgets, you could explore launching such products. Staying adaptable helps maintain relevance even if traditional gadgets face declining demand.

2. Handling Credit Risk:

Implement a credit control policy. For **TechZone**, this could mean offering a **2%** discount for customers who pay within **10 days**. If ₹**1,00,000** worth of sales take advantage of this, you'll receive ₹**98,000** upfront, which improves cash flow.

3. Reducing Liquidity Risk:

Maintaining a cash reserve or a line of credit ensures you have funds during low-cash months. If **TechZone** sets aside ₹**50,000** monthly, you'll have ₹**6,00,000** by year's end, which can cover unexpected expenses and smooth out cash flow.

4. Mitigating Operational Risk:

Regular equipment maintenance and cross-training employees can reduce disruptions. For example, if **TechZone** sets aside ₹**20,000** annually for maintenance, it helps prevent larger costs associated with major breakdowns. Additionally, having a backup supplier can reduce downtime if your primary supplier faces issues.

5. Addressing Interest Rate Risk:

Consider locking in fixed rates for loans. If **TechZone** locks in a **10%** rate on a ₹**10,00,000** loan, you know your annual cost is ₹**1,00,000**. This protects you from the uncertainty of variable rates, making financial planning easier.

6. Managing Foreign Exchange Risk:

Hedge foreign exchange risk with forward contracts. If **TechZone** signs a contract to lock in ₹78 per dollar for a **$10,000** order, your cost remains **₹7,80,000**, regardless of future currency fluctuations. This helps maintain predictable costs.

7. Mitigating Compliance Risk:

Consult with tax and legal advisors to ensure **TechZone** meets all regulations. Regular internal audits can help avoid penalties. For example, budgeting **₹25,000** annually for compliance reviews may save you from paying larger fines later.

Vinu: These strategies are really helpful, but what happens if something goes wrong despite all these precautions?

Manu: Great question, Vinu. Even with the best risk management strategies, things can still go wrong. That's why it's essential to have a **contingency plan** and **risk response strategy** ready.

Step 3: Building Contingency Plans and Staying Resilient

1. Creating a Contingency Plan:

For each risk, have a backup plan. If a key supplier fails, **TechZone** should have a list of alternative suppliers who can step in. If you face cash flow problems, a pre-approved credit line of **₹2,00,000** can help you cover immediate expenses without scrambling for funds.

2. Monitoring Risks Regularly:

Risk management is an ongoing process. For **TechZone**, review financial performance and industry trends quarterly to identify new risks. For example, track customer payment patterns—if delays increase, it might be time to tighten credit terms.

3. Using Insurance as a Safety Net:

Business insurance can cover unexpected losses. If **TechZone** has ₹1,00,000 worth of stock and buys insurance against theft or damage, you're protected if something goes wrong. It's an additional layer of security.

4. Effective Communication in Crisis:

In a crisis, communicate clearly with your team, customers, and suppliers. If **TechZone** faces a product shortage, notify customers promptly and offer alternatives, like pre-orders. This maintains customer trust even during tough times.

5. Regular Risk Assessments and Adapting Strategies:

As **TechZone** grows, so do the risks. Reassess regularly and adapt. If you introduce a new product line, consider any unique risks that come with it, like needing additional safety certifications or ensuring reliable supply sources.

Vinu: It sounds like the key is to be prepared for anything that might happen and to keep evaluating risks as **TechZone** grows. Is there anything else I should consider?

Manu: Yes, Vinu. The main idea is to keep risk management as a continuous process. This way, you're not just protecting **TechZone** but also positioning it to thrive under different circumstances. As you expand, these risk management strategies will help ensure stability and resilience.

7.2 Financial Governance and Internal Controls

Vinu: Manu, I keep hearing about how important it is to have financial governance and internal controls in place, and I need guidance on where to start. With **TechZone** growing, I want to make sure everything stays transparent and protected, but I don't know what specific steps I need to take to ensure financial integrity. Can you guide me through this?

Manu: Of course, Vinu! Financial governance and internal controls are essential as your business grows. They're like the backbone of a well-run organization, helping to prevent fraud, ensure transparency, and protect your assets. For **TechZone**, putting these controls in place will ensure that finances are managed responsibly as you expand.

Let's break this down so you can implement these practices step by step and align them with TechZone's growth.

Understanding Financial Governance

Manu: Financial governance is about establishing a set of rules, policies, and processes that govern how your business handles finances. This keeps everything transparent and aligned with your business goals. Here's why it's essential:

1. Preventing Fraud:

Clear financial policies minimize opportunities for fraud. For example, if **TechZone** has policies limiting how funds are accessed and spent, it's harder for someone to misuse them.

2. Ensuring Accuracy and Transparency:

Good financial governance gives you a clear picture of your finances. Imagine if **TechZone** has ₹10,00,000 in revenue each month, but without clear tracking, it's hard to know where every rupee is going. Governance makes sure every amount is accounted for.

3. Compliance with Regulations:

Staying compliant with tax regulations or industry rules is critical. If **TechZone** fails to adhere to financial regulations, it could face fines or penalties that could impact your profitability.

4. Supporting Strategic Growth:

With a solid governance framework, you'll know exactly how resources are being used. This enables better decision-making, like determining whether **TechZone** can afford an expansion or a new product line.

Vinu: So, financial governance gives me a framework to ensure that finances are handled properly, which helps protect **TechZone** from fraud or mismanagement. But what about internal controls?

Establishing Internal Controls

Manu: Internal controls are the specific processes you put in place to monitor, safeguard, and verify financial transactions. They're the practical steps that support financial governance. Here's how they work:

1. Segregation of Duties:

No single person should handle every part of a financial transaction. For example, if **TechZone** has one person responsible for both authorizing and processing payments, it's easier for fraud to occur. Splitting duties—for example, having one person approve a **₹20,000** payment and another process it—reduces this risk.

2. Authorization and Approvals:

Set approval limits based on transaction size. For instance, at TechZone, you might require your approval for any expense over ₹50,000, while department heads can approve amounts under ₹10,000. This ensures larger expenses get multiple levels of review.

3. Documented Procedures:

Every financial process, like payroll or expense claims, should have a documented process. For instance, if employees at **TechZone** need to submit expenses, they should follow a specific process to ensure all details are captured correctly. This helps with consistency and minimizes errors.

4. Regular Reconciliations:

Regularly comparing financial records, like bank statements with internal accounts, is crucial. Suppose **TechZone** has a monthly reconciliation where bank records are compared to sales. If you notice ₹30,000 unaccounted for, you can investigate and resolve it promptly.

5. Access Controls:

Only authorized personnel should access sensitive financial information. At **TechZone**, this might mean that only you and your accountant have full access to the accounting system, while others see only what's relevant to their roles. This keeps data secure and reduces the risk of unauthorized changes.

Vinu: That makes sense. Internal controls ensure that no single person has too much control over any financial transaction and that everything is properly managed. How should I implement these controls at TechZone?

Implementing Controls at TechZone

Manu: Here's how you can start implementing these internal controls:

1. Set Clear Approval Limits:

Define spending thresholds. For instance, if **TechZone** sets a rule where expenses under ₹10,000 can be approved by department heads but anything over ₹50,000 needs both your approval and the CFO's, it adds layers of accountability for larger expenses.

2. Implement Monthly Reconciliations:

Have someone in your team reconcile the bank accounts with your records every month. Suppose **TechZone** receives ₹4,50,000 in sales but sees only

₹4,30,000 credited to the bank. Monthly reconciliations would highlight this ₹20,000 difference so you can address it quickly.

3. Use Accounting Software for Tracking:

Investing in software can help you monitor approvals and set up alerts for unusual transactions. For example, **TechZone** could set up a rule where the system flags any expense over ₹25,000, prompting you to review it. This automation reduces the chance of errors slipping through.

4. Limit Access to Sensitive Data:

Only give access to financial information on a need-to-know basis. In **TechZone**, department heads might have access to their budget data, but only the finance team sees the entire financial picture. This control limits potential data leaks or unauthorized changes.

5. Conduct Internal Audits:

Regularly audit key processes. You don't have to make it formal initially— just review a few transactions each month to check that the correct approvals were obtained. For example, if **TechZone** had an ₹80,000 equipment purchase, auditing would ensure all the necessary steps were followed.

Vinu: That's helpful! So, by setting approval limits, conducting reconciliations, and using software, I can protect TechZone'sfinances. What about preventing fraud specifically?

Preventing Fraud with Internal Controls

Manu: Internal controls are your best defense against fraud. Here's how they work:

1. Segregation of Duties:

By ensuring one person doesn't handle all parts of a transaction, you create a system of checks and balances. For example, if an employee at **TechZone** authorizes and processes a ₹15,000 payment, they could misappropriate funds. Having separate people handle these steps reduces this risk.

2. Regular Reconciliation:

Comparing bank statements with internal records can reveal fraud. If **TechZone** finds that ₹50,000 is missing during a reconciliation, it's a sign to investigate. By doing this monthly, you can catch issues before they escalate.

3. Approval Workflows:

Having multiple approvals, especially for large payments, makes unauthorized transactions difficult. Suppose **TechZone** requires two sign-offs for expenses over ₹1,00,000. This means one person can't approve high-value payments without someone else's knowledge.

4. Access Control:

Restrict access to sensitive financial data. For instance, if only a few trusted employees at **TechZone** can make entries in your accounting system, it reduces the risk of unauthorized transactions.

5. Monitoring Unusual Transactions:

With the right controls, you can track and investigate unusual activity. If **TechZone** suddenly has a spike in petty cash usage, for instance, you can investigate and take action.

Vinu: It sounds like these controls not only protect **TechZone** from fraud but also ensure we're compliant with legal requirements. Is there more I should know about compliance?

Ensuring Compliance

Manu: Compliance is another critical area that internal controls support. Here's how they keep **TechZone** compliant with laws and regulations:

1. Tax Compliance:

Accurate record-keeping is essential for tax purposes. For example, by having documented processes for tracking ₹5,00,000 in monthly revenue and ₹2,00,000 in expenses, you'll have a clear record when it's time to file taxes.

2. Regulatory Reporting:

If **TechZone** is in an industry that requires specific financial reporting, having controls ensures you meet these requirements. For example, accounting standards might require particular revenue recognition methods. Your controls can ensure these are followed.

3. Audit Trails:

Strong internal controls create a clear audit trail. If **TechZone** is ever audited, you'll have documentation showing every step of each transaction—who approved it, who processed it, and why. This transparency is essential for proving that **TechZone** complies with the law.

Vinu: It sounds like financial governance and internal controls not only protect **TechZone** from fraud but also ensure everything's legal and above board. This definitely gives me peace of mind as we grow.

Manu: Exactly, Vinu! Implementing financial governance and internal controls creates a solid foundation for **TechZone** to grow confidently, knowing your finances are protected and transparent. With these practices in place, you'll have a robust framework that supports growth, compliance, and trust across your business.

Chapter 8 - Tax Planning and Compliance

Vinu: Manu, I've always found taxes a bit overwhelming. I know that staying compliant with tax regulations is crucial for **TechZone**, but I also hear about the importance of **tax planning** to minimize liabilities. I want to make sure I'm not paying more than necessary while avoiding any trouble with tax authorities. Can you explain how to approach this?

Manu: Absolutely, Vinu! **Tax planning and compliance** are essential for running a healthy business. While taxes can feel overwhelming, with the right approach, you can stay compliant with tax regulations while also minimizing your tax liabilities—legally, of course. It's all about understanding the rules, using them to your advantage, and making sure **TechZone** is on solid ground with the tax authorities.

Let's break this down step by step, so you can see how tax planning and compliance work together.

What is Tax Compliance?

Manu: First, let's talk about **tax compliance**. This is the foundation—you need to ensure that **TechZone** follows all applicable tax laws, files returns on time, and pays the correct amount of taxes. It's non-negotiable, and any mistake here can lead to penalties or even legal issues. Here's what tax compliance involves:

1. Filing Returns on Time:

The most basic part of compliance is filing your tax returns on time. Depending on the size and nature of your business, **TechZone** will have deadlines for **Income tax, GST, TDS (Tax Deducted at Source),** and possibly other types of taxes. Missing these deadlines can result in fines and penalties.

2. Accurate Record Keeping:

Tax compliance also means maintaining accurate financial records. You need to have a clear record of all your **income**, **expenses**, and **deductions**. For **TechZone**, this means ensuring that every sale, expense, and investment is properly documented. If the tax authorities ever audit you, accurate records will protect you from any discrepancies.

4. Paying the Right Taxes:

This includes calculating the correct amount of tax to be paid—whether it's corporate income tax, GST, or any other tax your business is liable for. Underpaying can result in penalties, and overpaying means you're tying up valuable cash unnecessarily.

Vinu: Okay, so compliance is about making sure I'm following the rules, filing everything on time, and keeping accurate records. But what about **tax planning**—how does that help me save on taxes?

What is Tax Planning?

Manu: Great question! **Tax planning** is the process of strategically arranging your finances and business activities in a way that minimizes your tax liabilities while staying fully compliant with the law. It's about making smart decisions that reduce your tax burden, leaving more money for **TechZone** to reinvest in growth.

Here are the key elements of tax planning:

1. Making Use of Deductions:

One of the best ways to minimize taxes is by claiming **legitimate deductions**. These are expenses that the tax authorities allow you to subtract from your taxable income, which lowers the amount of tax you owe. For **TechZone**, this might include:

- **Business expenses**, like rent, salaries, utilities, and office supplies.
- **Depreciation** on equipment and machinery.
- **Interest on loans** that are used for business purposes.

By making sure you claim every allowable deduction, you'll reduce your taxable income and, therefore, the amount of tax you owe.

2. Using Tax Credits:

Tax credits are even better than deductions because they directly reduce the amount of tax you owe, rather than just lowering your taxable income. Depending on your location, **TechZone** may be eligible for credits related to R&D (Research and Development), environmental initiatives, or hiring certain types of employees. Make sure to explore whether there are any credits that could apply to your business.

3. Structuring Business Investments Smartly:

How you invest your business's money also affects your tax liabilities. For example, if **TechZone** purchases new equipment, you can usually claim **depreciation** on that equipment, spreading the cost over several years and reducing your taxable income each year. Strategic investments in certain assets can offer significant tax benefits.

4. Tax-Efficient Business Structure:

Sometimes, the **structure** of your business can impact how much tax you pay. For instance, there might be tax advantages to registering as an LLP (Limited Liability Partnership) instead of a sole proprietorship, or even forming a private limited company. This decision should be based on how **TechZone** is growing, and you might want to consult with a tax advisor to see if restructuring could lower your overall tax burden.

5. Timing of Expenses and Income:

Another key part of tax planning is the **timing** of your expenses and income. For example, if **TechZone** is expecting to make a large profit in the current financial year, you might accelerate some planned expenses (like buying new equipment or prepaying for services) before the year ends. This way, you can reduce your taxable income for the current year.

Vinu: That makes sense. So, tax planning is about using deductions, credits, and structuring my expenses to reduce how much tax I owe. But how do I balance that with compliance, so I'm not crossing any lines?

Manu: Exactly! The key is to strike a balance between **minimizing taxes** and staying fully compliant. The best tax planning strategies are the ones that take advantage of legal **loopholes** and opportunities, without ever stepping into grey areas that could get you in trouble with the tax authorities.

Here's how you can balance both:

1. Know the Rules:

Make sure you have a strong understanding of the tax laws and regulations that apply to **TechZone**. If you're not sure about something, consult a tax professional who can advise you on how to structure your finances in a way that maximizes savings while keeping you within the legal boundaries.

2. Stay Transparent:

Don't try to hide anything from the tax authorities. While tax planning helps you reduce your liabilities, it should always be done **transparently**. For example, if you're claiming deductions or credits, make sure you have proper documentation for every claim. If there's ever an audit, transparency will protect you.

3. Monitor Changes in Tax Laws:

Tax laws can change from year to year, so it's important to **stay up to date** with any new regulations or amendments. If the government introduces new tax credits, or changes the rules around certain deductions, you'll want to take advantage of these changes. For example, if new tax incentives are introduced for businesses investing in technology, **TechZone** can benefit by planning investments accordingly.

4. Create a Tax Plan Early:

Tax planning shouldn't be done at the last minute. You should have a **year-round tax strategy** that looks at how you can structure your finances to reduce taxes well before the tax season begins. This means making decisions early—such as timing expenses, considering asset purchases, or restructuring your business—to ensure you get the maximum benefit when it's time to file.

Vinu: So, as long as I'm being transparent, following the rules, and planning ahead, I can take advantage of tax-saving strategies without worrying about non-compliance?

Manu: Exactly. With the right balance, **TechZone** can save a significant amount of money through tax planning, while also staying on the right side of the law.

Manu: Let's talk about how you can apply these strategies specifically to **TechZone**. Here's a step-by-step approach to getting started with tax planning and compliance:

1. Keep Detailed Records:

Make sure **TechZone** maintains meticulous financial records. This includes keeping receipts for every expense, maintaining accurate sales records, and documenting every transaction. You'll need these records when claiming deductions or if you're ever audited.

2. Track Business Expenses Carefully:

Review all your expenses and see what qualifies for deductions. For TechZone, this could include things like:

- **Office rent** and utilities.

- **Employee salaries** and benefits.

- **Business travel** and client entertainment.

- **Advertising and marketing expenses.**

The more business-related expenses you can claim, the lower your taxable income will be.

4. Depreciate Assets Over Time:

If **TechZone** has invested in equipment or machinery, you can spread the cost over several years through **depreciation**. This reduces your taxable income each year, rather than taking a one-time hit to profits. For example, if you buy equipment worth ₹10,00,000, you could depreciate it over 5 years, lowering your taxable income each year.

5. Plan for the Long Term:

Consider your **long-term tax strategy**. For example, if you're planning to expand **TechZone** or invest in a new product line, look into whether there are tax incentives for research and development, or for creating jobs. By planning ahead, you can make strategic decisions that reduce your tax burden over time.

6. Consult with a Tax Professional:

Finally, work with a **tax advisor** to review your tax strategy regularly. They can help you identify opportunities you might not have considered and ensure you're taking advantage of all the deductions and credits available to **TechZone**. A tax advisor can also help you navigate any changes in tax laws that might affect your business.

Vinu: That's really helpful, Manu. I feel much clearer on how to approach taxes now. By planning ahead, using deductions and credits, and keeping detailed records, I can make sure **TechZone** isn't paying more than it needs to while staying compliant with the tax authorities.

Manu: Exactly, Vinu! When you take the time to plan your taxes properly, it's not just about avoiding penalties—it's about keeping more of your money so you can reinvest in **TechZone**. With a smart tax strategy in place, you'll be able to use that saved capital to **grow your business.**

Chapter 9 - Strategic Financial Decisions

9.1 Funding Options and Access to Capital

Vinu: Manu, as **TechZone** continues to grow, I'm starting to realize that I'll need additional capital to fund expansion, new product lines, or even just to manage cash flow more effectively. I know there are different ways to raise funds, like taking on debt or finding investors, but I'm not sure which option is best for **TechZone's** short-term and long-term needs. Can you help me figure out what the best funding options are?

Manu: Absolutely, Vinu! Finding the right **funding** option for **TechZone** is crucial because the way you raise capital can have a significant impact on the future of your business. Whether you need capital to fund a new project, expand operations, or manage cash flow, you'll want to explore different **financing options** to find the one that aligns with your short-term needs and long-term goals.

Let's break it down and go over the **debt**, **equity**, and other financing sources available to you, and when each might be the best fit for **TechZone**.

Short-Term Funding Options

Manu: Let's start by discussing **short-term funding**, which is typically used to meet immediate needs like managing working capital, covering short-term expenses, or dealing with unexpected cash flow issues. Here are some common short-term funding options:

1. Business Line of Credit:

A **line of credit** is one of the most flexible options for short-term funding. It allows you to borrow up to a certain limit, and you only pay interest on the amount you actually use. This is great for covering short-term needs like inventory purchases or payroll. For **TechZone**, having a line of credit could help you manage fluctuations in cash flow, especially during busy seasons or when you're waiting for payments from customers.

2. Short-Term Loans:

These are loans that you repay within a year or less. They're ideal for covering specific short-term needs, such as buying equipment or making small upgrades. The advantage is that you get a lump sum of cash upfront, but you'll need to repay it relatively quickly, often with higher interest rates. For **TechZone**, if you need a small infusion of cash to finance a new marketing campaign or purchase extra inventory for a big sales season, a short-term loan might be a good option.

3. Invoice Financing (Factoring):

If you have customers who pay on credit terms, **invoice financing** allows you to access cash based on your outstanding invoices. A lender advances you a percentage of the invoice amount, and you repay it when your customers pay their invoices. This is helpful when you need to bridge the gap between delivering products and receiving payments. For **TechZone**, if you have large unpaid invoices but need immediate cash for operations, invoice financing could be a useful tool.

4. Trade Credit:

Trade credit is when your suppliers allow you to pay for goods or services at a later date, usually 30 to 90 days after the invoice is issued. It's essentially an interest-free loan from your suppliers. If **TechZone** can negotiate favorable payment terms with suppliers, this can help you preserve cash in the short term without taking on formal debt.

Vinu: That makes sense. So for short-term needs like managing cash flow or covering immediate expenses, options like a line of credit or short-term loans give me flexibility without committing to long-term debt. But what if I'm thinking about longer-term growth or a major expansion?

Long-Term Funding Options

Manu: Exactly. For **long-term growth**—like opening a new location, investing in significant equipment, or launching new products—you'll want to look at financing options that provide larger amounts of capital over longer repayment periods. Here are some long-term funding options:

1. Term Loans:

A **term loan** is a traditional loan where you borrow a lump sum and repay it over several years with interest. These loans are usually used for major investments, such as purchasing property, expanding operations, or buying expensive equipment. For **TechZone**, if you're looking to open a new location or make a big investment in technology, a term loan with a fixed interest rate and predictable payments could be a good fit.

2. Equipment Financing:

If **TechZone** needs to invest in new machinery or technology, **equipment financing** allows you to borrow money specifically to purchase those assets. The asset itself serves as collateral, which often makes the terms more favorable. The loan is repaid over the useful life of the equipment. This is a great way to fund big-ticket purchases without having to pay the full amount upfront.

3. Commercial Real Estate Loans:

If you're planning to buy property for **TechZone**, such as a new office or warehouse, a **commercial real estate loan** can help finance the purchase. These loans typically have longer repayment terms, often 10 to 25 years. The property itself serves as collateral, which can lower the interest rates compared to unsecured loans.

4. Equity Financing:

Equity financing involves raising money by selling a portion of your business to investors in exchange for capital. This is a common way for startups and high-growth companies to raise large sums of money without taking on debt. The trade-off, of course, is that you give up some ownership and control. If **TechZone** is looking to raise a significant amount of money for expansion, you might consider bringing on equity investors who can also offer expertise and industry connections.

5. Venture Capital or Angel Investors:

Similar to equity financing, **venture capital** or **angel investors** provide funding in exchange for equity in your company. The difference is that these investors often target businesses with high growth potential and are willing to take on more risk. If **TechZone** has a scalable business model and you're looking for rapid growth, venture capital or angel funding might be worth exploring.

Vinu: I've heard a lot about venture capital, but I'm a bit concerned about giving up control of the business. Are there other ways to raise long-term capital without giving up equity?

Other Sources of Capital

Manu: Great point! There are indeed other ways to raise capital without diluting your ownership. Here are a few alternatives:

1. Crowdfunding:

Crowdfunding platforms allow you to raise money from a large number of people, typically in exchange for early access to products or perks rather than equity. This can be a great way to finance new product lines for **TechZone** without giving up control. However, it requires a strong marketing effort and a compelling story to attract backers.Crowdfunding is particularly effective if you have a product that resonates with a broad audience.

2. Government Grants and Subsidies:

There are various **government grants and subsidies** available, especially for businesses in sectors like **technology, innovation, and sustainability**. For example, programs offered by the **Ministry of Micro, Small, and Medium Enterprises (MSME), Startup programs,** and **Digital initiatives** provide funding and incentives for eligible businesses. TechZone could explore these avenues, as many of these grants are designed to support tech-focused businesses and may not require repayment.

3. Revenue-Based Financing (RBF):

Revenue-based financing allows businesses to receive capital in exchange for a percentage of future revenue. This is a flexible option if **TechZone** has consistent sales, as repayments are tied directly to your monthly revenue. Unlike traditional loans, RBF doesn't have fixed monthly payments; instead, the amount varies depending on your revenue. This flexibility can be beneficial, especially when revenue fluctuates seasonally or due to market conditions.

4. Peer-to-Peer (P2P) Lending:

Peer-to-peer lending platforms connect businesses directly with individual investors willing to provide loans. Often, these platforms can offer more competitive terms compared to traditional banks, especially if TechZone has a strong business plan and solid financials. P2P lending is a good choice if you need quick access to funds and prefer a relatively simple application process.

Vinu: That's a lot of options! It seems like there's no one-size-fits-all solution. How do I know which funding option is right for **TechZone**, especially when balancing short-term and long-term needs?

Choosing the Right Funding Option for TechZone

Manu: You're right—there's no one-size-fits-all solution. The best funding option for **TechZone** depends on several factors:

1. Purpose of the Funds:

What do you need the funds for? If it's for **working capital** or **short-term cash flow**, a line of credit or short-term loan might be best. If it's for **long-term growth**—like expanding to a new location or investing in major equipment—then a term loan or equity financing might make more sense.

2. Cost of Capital:

Each funding option comes with its own costs, including **interest rates** for debt or giving up **equity** in the case of investors. You'll need to weigh the **cost of capital** against the potential return on investment. For example, if taking on debt helps you grow and increase profits, the interest you pay might be worth it. But if giving up equity results in losing too much control, you may want to avoid that route.

3. Repayment Flexibility:

Consider how flexible you need repayment terms to be. Debt typically requires fixed repayments, while equity financing doesn't involve repayment but does involve giving up ownership. If **TechZone** has seasonal sales or fluctuating cash flow, you might need a funding option that offers more flexibility, such as revenue-based financing or a line of credit.

4. Control Over the Business:

How much control are you willing to give up? If maintaining full control is important, then **debt financing** is likely a better option than equity financing. But if you're open to bringing on partners who can also provide strategic value, **venture capital** or **angel investment** might be worth considering.

5. Business Growth Stage:

Where is **TechZone** in its growth journey? If you're still in the early stages, you might rely more on **personal savings**, **bootstrapping,** or **angel investors**. As **TechZone** grows, you'll have access to more traditional financing options, like **bank loans** or even **IPO** (Initial Public Offering) if you scale significantly.

Vinu: That really helps clarify things. So, I need to think about what the funds will be used for, how much control I'm willing to give up, and the overall cost of the financing. It sounds like I might need a mix of options depending on whether I'm dealing with short-term or long-term needs.

Manu: Exactly! Often, businesses use a **combination of funding options** to meet both short-term and long-term needs. For **TechZone**, you might start with a **line of credit** to manage cash flow, while **exploring term loans** or **equity financing** for larger growth projects. The key is to stay flexible and adapt your funding strategy as your business evolves.

9.2 Profit Distribution and Reinvestment

Vinu: Manu, now that **TechZone** is starting to generate consistent profits, I've been thinking about what to do with them. Should I **reinvest** all the profits back into the business to fuel growth, or should I start **distributing** some of the profits to myself and other stakeholders? How do I strike the right balance between these two?

Manu: That's a great question, Vinu! Deciding what to do with your profits is a critical part of managing a growing business. Striking a balance between **reinvesting** in **TechZone** and **distributing** profits to stakeholders is important for both the long-term growth of the business and keeping everyone involved satisfied.

Let's go over why both reinvestment and profit distribution are important, and how you can find the right balance.

Manu: Reinvesting profits means putting some of your earnings back into the business to fuel **growth** and improve **efficiency**. It's an essential strategy for businesses that want to expand, stay competitive, or even innovate in the market. Here's why reinvestment is crucial for TechZone:

1. Funding Growth Initiatives:

Reinvesting profits allows you to fund **growth projects** without needing to rely on external financing like loans or equity. For **TechZone**, this could mean expanding to new locations, launching new product lines, or investing in marketing to reach more customers.

2. Upgrading Technology or Equipment:

As **TechZone** grows, your infrastructure may need upgrades. Reinvesting profits into new **technology, software,** or **equipment** can increase productivity and reduce long-term operational costs. For example, buying more efficient manufacturing equipment or investing in automation can help you produce gadgets faster and at a lower cost.

3. Increasing Working Capital:

Reinvestment can help build **working capital**, which gives you more flexibility to manage day-to-day operations, cover payroll, or buy inventory without needing to rely on short-term loans. Having a healthy buffer of working capital allows **TechZone** to operate smoothly, even when cash flow fluctuates.

4. Strengthening the Business's Financial Health:

Reinvesting profits also helps **strengthen the financial health** of your business. The more profit you reinvest, the more you build up your company's reserves. This financial strength makes it easier to secure loans or attract investors in the future, as **TechZone** will be seen as a stable and growing business.

Vinu: So reinvesting profits helps **TechZone** grow and stay competitive by funding expansion and improving operations. But what about distributing profits—why is that important?

Why Profit Distribution is Important for Stakeholders

Manu: Distributing profits is equally important because it **rewards stakeholders** for their investment in the business. Whether it's you as the owner, other partners, or shareholders, **profit distribution** shows that the business is performing well and sharing the benefits with those involved. Here's why it matters:

1. Rewarding Yourself and Partners:

As the owner of **TechZone**, you've put in a lot of hard work, and distributing profits is your reward for that effort. Profit distributions allow you to take money out of the business for personal use or reinvest in other ventures. It's also a way to reward any partners or investors who have helped build the business, keeping them motivated and committed to the company's success.

2. Maintaining Stakeholder Confidence:

Regular profit distributions can help **maintain confidence** among stakeholders. If you have investors, they'll expect to see returns on their investment, and regular distributions show that **TechZone** is financially stable and generating value. For example, if you've taken on equity investors, paying out a portion of the profits keeps them happy and invested in the long-term success of the business.

3. Building Trust and Retaining Talent:

Distributing profits can also be a way to **build trust** within your team. If you have key employees or partners who hold shares or have a stake in the business, offering them profit shares or bonuses shows that you value their contribution. It can be a powerful tool for retaining top talent and keeping everyone motivated to grow **TechZone**.

4. Personal Financial Goals:

Don't forget your own personal financial goals. By distributing some of the profits, you can diversify your investments, plan for your future, and ensure financial security outside of the business. While reinvestment is important, you also need to think about how **TechZone** fits into your broader financial life.

Vinu: That makes sense. So, profit distribution isn't just about taking money out of the business—it also helps maintain **stakeholder confidence** and shows that the business is delivering value. How do I decide how much to reinvest and how much to distribute?

Striking the Balance Between Reinvestment and Profit Distribution

Manu: The balance between **reinvestment** and **profit distribution** depends on several factors, including **TechZone's growth stage**, your **business goals,** and your **personal financial needs**. Here's how you can approach it:

1. Assess Your Growth Plans:

First, consider **TechZone's growth trajectory**. If you're in a high-growth phase where you need capital for expansion, new product development, or market penetration, it makes sense to reinvest a larger portion of your profits. On the other hand, if growth is steady and you don't have immediate large-scale projects, you can afford to distribute more profits to yourself and other stakeholders.

2. Consider Business Needs First:

Before distributing profits, ensure that **TechZone** has enough capital to cover operational needs, working capital, and any upcoming investments. You don't want to distribute profits only to find that you're short on cash to fund day-to-day activities or growth opportunities. For example, if you're planning to launch a new product line, reinvesting a significant portion of profits might be necessary to finance that.

3. Reinvest for Long-Term Stability:

Even if **TechZone** is doing well, you should always reinvest a portion of your profits to ensure long-term stability. Building **financial reserves** or investing in technology, marketing, or talent can help you future-proof the business and ensure continued success. Think of this as setting the foundation for sustained growth, rather than focusing solely on short-term gains.

4. Set Profit Distribution Targets:

Once you've assessed your business's needs, you can set a **target** for how much profit to distribute. For example, you might decide to distribute 30-40% of the profits to yourself and other stakeholders, while reinvesting the remaining 60-70% back into the business. The exact ratio will depend on **TechZone's** current stage and how much capital you need for future growth.

5. Be Flexible:

The ratio between reinvestment and distribution doesn't have to be set in stone. It's okay to be **flexible** and adjust the balance as your business evolves. For instance, in a year where **TechZone** has a significant expansion opportunity, you might reinvest a higher percentage of profits. In more stable years, you can distribute more to reward yourself and other stakeholders.

Vinu: I like the idea of setting a target for distribution but keeping some flexibility depending on the business's needs. But how do I know when it's time to increase distributions or shift more toward reinvestment?

When to Shift Between Reinvestment and Profit Distribution

Manu: Good question, Vinu! The balance between reinvestment and distribution may shift over time based on **TechZone'sperformance**, growth opportunities, and your financial situation. Here's how you can determine when it's time to adjust:

1. When Growth Opportunities Arise:

If a **new growth opportunity** presents itself—like entering a new market, launching a new product, or acquiring another business—it's wise to prioritize reinvestment. This allows you to seize those opportunities without relying on external funding. For example, if a new gadget trend emerges and **TechZone** wants to be one of the first to market, reinvesting more profits would allow you to act quickly.

2. When Business Maturity Increases:

As **TechZone** matures and growth stabilizes, you may find that your need for large-scale reinvestment decreases. At this point, you can increase profit distributions, rewarding yourself and other stakeholders for the hard work put into growing the business. This is common in businesses that are past the rapid expansion phase and generating **steady cash flow**.

3. When Cash Reserves Are Strong:

If **TechZone** has built up **healthy cash reserves** and can cover both day-to-day operations and future investments, it may be time to distribute more profits. A strong cash position means you have enough capital on hand for any unexpected expenses or opportunities, allowing you to safely distribute more of the profits.

4. When Stakeholders Expect Returns:

If **TechZone** has equity investors or partners who expect returns, you'll need to balance **reinvesting for growth** with **distributing profits** to meet their expectations. Regular, predictable profit distributions help maintain investor confidence and keep them satisfied, especially if they've been waiting for a return on their investment.

5. Personal Financial Needs:

Lastly, consider your own **financial goals**. If you've reached a stage where you need to start taking more profits out of **TechZone** for personal financial planning—whether for retirement, buying a home, or investing in other ventures—you can adjust your strategy to distribute a higher percentage of profits while ensuring the business remains healthy.

Vinu: So, it's really about balancing the needs of the business with the expectations of stakeholders and my own financial goals. I can see how this will evolve over time as **TechZone** grows.

Manu: Exactly! By being strategic and flexible, you can strike the right balance between **reinvesting** for growth and **distributing profits** to reward yourself and others. It's all about ensuring the long-term success of **TechZone** while also enjoying the fruits of your hard work.

9.3 Exit Strategy and Valuation

Vinu: Manu, as I think about the long-term future of **TechZone**, I realize that at some point I might want to either **sell** the business, **pass it on** to someone else, or even **step back** and let others run it. But I'm not sure how to plan for an **exit strategy**, or how to figure out what **TechZone** would be worth if I wanted to sell it. How do I approach this?

Manu: That's a great question, Vinu! Planning an **exit strategy** is a crucial part of building a business, even if you're not thinking about exiting anytime soon. It gives you control over what happens to **TechZone** in the future, whether you sell it, pass it on, or step back from day-to-day operations. Understanding your **business valuation** is also key because it helps you know what your business is worth when the time comes to consider an exit.

Let's walk through the steps to plan your **exit strategy** and how to approach **valuing your business** for that eventual day.

What is an Exit Strategy?

Manu: An **exit strategy** is your long-term plan for what will happen to your business when you decide to step away. It could involve selling the business, passing it on to a family member, or having a management team take over. Planning your exit early gives you options and allows you to maximize the value you get when you eventually step back. Here are some common types of exit strategies:

1. Selling the Business:

This is one of the most common exit strategies. You sell **TechZone** to an outside buyer—either another company, a private equity firm, or an individual. The goal is to sell it at a price that reflects the value of all the hard work and growth you've built over the years.

2. Passing the Business to a Successor:

If you want to keep **TechZone** within the family or pass it on to a key employee, you can create a **succession plan**. This involves identifying a successor who can take over management and ownership of the business when you're ready to step back.

3. Mergers and Acquisitions (M&A):

In this strategy, **TechZone** merges with or is acquired by another business. This can often result in a higher sale price, especially if the acquiring company is looking to enter your market or expand its operations. Mergers and acquisitions are common in industries where consolidation is happening.

4. Management Buyout (MBO):

In a **management buyout**, the existing management team purchases the business from you. This is a good option if you have a strong management team in place that wants to continue running the business. You exit the business, but it stays under the control of people who know it well.

5. Initial Public Offering (IPO):

For larger businesses with high growth potential, an **IPO** might be an option. This involves offering shares of **TechZone** to the public on a stock exchange. While it's less common for small to medium-sized businesses, it's a possible exit strategy if your business grows significantly.

6. Liquidation:

In some cases, business owners choose to **liquidate** their assets and close the business. This isn't ideal if you want to maximize the value of your business, but it can be an option if you don't want to continue running it and there's no clear buyer or successor.

Vinu: That's really helpful! So, an exit strategy could involve selling the business, passing it on, or even merging with another company. How do I know which strategy is right for **TechZone**?

Manu: Choosing the right exit strategy depends on your **personal goals,** the **business's financial health,** and the **market conditions** at the time you're considering an exit. Here's how to think through it:

1. What Are Your Long-Term Goals?

If your goal is to **retire** and cash out, selling the business or going through an acquisition might be the best option. On the other hand, if you want **TechZone** to continue running under a trusted team, a **management buyout** or **succession plan** might make more sense. Think about what's most important to you—getting the highest sale price, ensuring the business's legacy, or maintaining control in some capacity.

2. Is There a Successor in Mind?

If you have a family member or key employee who could take over, you might prefer to pass the business on to them through a **succession plan**. This requires training the successor early, so they're ready to step into your shoes when the time comes.

3. Current Market Conditions:

The **market environment** also plays a big role in choosing the right exit strategy. For example, if your industry is going through a period of consolidation, **merging with another company** could offer a lucrative exit. Or, if **TechZone** is in a high-growth industry, attracting outside buyers or venture capitalists might be easier.

4. The Financial Health of Your Business:

A strong, financially healthy business is easier to sell or pass on. If **TechZone** has solid financials, loyal customers, and growth potential, you'll have more options for a successful exit. However, if the business is struggling, you may need to focus on **turning it around** before you can implement a favorable exit strategy.

Vinu: That makes sense. I'll need to think about my long-term goals and how the business is performing before I choose an exit strategy. But how do I figure out how much **TechZone** is worth when the time comes to sell or pass it on?

Manu: That's the next crucial step—understanding the **valuation** of your business. Business valuation is the process of determining how much **TechZone** is worth in the market, and it's essential whether you're selling, passing it on, or merging with another company. Here are the key methods used to value a business:

1. Earnings Multiple (EBITDA or Net Income):

One of the most common ways to value a business is based on its **earnings**. For **TechZone**, this could be done using a multiple of your **EBITDA** (Earnings Before Interest, Taxes, Depreciation, and Amortization) or **net income**. The multiple is typically determined by the industry average and market conditions. For example, if the average multiple for businesses in your industry is 5x EBITDA, and **TechZone** has an EBITDA of ₹10,00,000, the business could be valued at ₹50,00,000.

2. Revenue Multiple:

Some businesses are valued based on a **multiple of revenue**. This is especially common in fast-growing industries where earnings might not fully capture the business's potential. For example, if **TechZone** generates ₹1 crore in revenue, and businesses in your industry are valued at 2x revenue, your business could be worth ₹2 crore. However, this method is often used for high-growth businesses with strong future potential.

3. Discounted Cash Flow (DCF) Analysis:

The **DCF method** values a business based on its future cash flows, discounted to present value. Essentially, it looks at how much **TechZone** is expected to generate in the future and adjusts that for the risk associated with achieving those cash flows. This method is often used for businesses with predictable and stable cash flows, and it can provide a detailed picture of the business's long-term value.

4. Asset-Based Valuation:

If **TechZone** owns significant **assets**—such as equipment, property, or intellectual property—an **asset-based valuation** might be appropriate. This method calculates the value of all the business's assets, minus its liabilities, to determine the **net worth** of the business. This method is more common for businesses in industries with high asset values, such as real estate or manufacturing.

5. Market Comparables (Comps):

Another method is to look at **comparable businesses** that have recently sold in your industry. This is called a **comparables (comps) analysis**. By looking at what similar businesses sold for, you can get a rough idea of what **TechZone** might be worth. This approach is useful when you have access to reliable data on recent transactions in your market.

Vinu: That's really helpful! So, I can value **TechZone** based on its **earnings**, **revenue**, or even the value of its **assets**, depending on the nature of the business. How do I choose the right valuation method?

Manu: The best **valuation method** depends on the nature of **TechZone's** business, the industry you're in, and the type of exit strategy you're pursuing. Here's how to choose:

1. If You're Selling to a Strategic Buyer:

If you're selling to a strategic buyer—like a competitor or a larger company looking to expand into your market—an **earnings multiple** (EBITDA or net income) or **revenue multiple** is often the most appropriate method. Strategic buyers are typically more interested in how much profit **TechZone** is generating or its future growth potential.

2. If You're Passing the Business On:

If you're passing **TechZone** on to a family member or key employee, you might use a **discounted cash flow (DCF)** analysis or an **asset-based valuation**. These methods ensure that the successor understands the future cash flows and the assets they're inheriting, giving them a clear picture of what the business is worth.

3. If You're Considering a Merger or Acquisition:

For mergers and acquisitions, buyers often look at **market comparables** (comps) to determine a fair valuation. By comparing **TechZone** to other similar businesses that have been acquired, you can get a realistic sense of what your business could fetch in a deal.

4. If You're Considering an IPO:

For an IPO, **TechZone** would likely be valued based on its **revenue** and **growth potential**, especially if you're in a high-growth industry. Public markets tend to favor businesses with strong revenue growth and market potential, even if they're not yet highly profitable.

Vinu: It sounds like the valuation method depends on the **buyer** and the **nature** of the exit strategy. Once I know the business's value, what steps do I need to take to make sure TechZone is ready for an exit?

Manu: Exactly! Once you've decided on your **exit strategy** and have a sense of the **valuation**, you'll need to start preparing **TechZone** for the transition. Here's how to make sure the business is ready:

1. Strengthen Financials:

Before you can exit, make sure **TechZone's financial records** are in top shape. This includes ensuring your profit and loss statements, balance sheets, and cash flow statements are accurate and up to date. Potential buyers or successors will want to see clean, well-organized financials that clearly show the business's profitability and potential for growth.

2. Streamline Operations:

Make sure your business runs smoothly without you. This means creating **standard operating procedures**(SOPs) for every part of the business—from sales and marketing to inventory management and customer service. This ensures that the business can continue operating effectively after you exit.

3. Build a Strong Management Team:

Having a strong **management team** in place is crucial for making the transition smoother. If potential buyers or successors see that **TechZone** can operate successfully without you, it increases the business's value. Consider training key employees to take on more responsibilities and preparing them to manage the business in your absence.

4. Legal and Compliance Matters:

Ensure that **TechZone** is fully compliant with all legal and regulatory requirements. This includes making sure your business licenses are up to date, contracts with suppliers and customers are in place, and any potential legal issues are resolved. A buyer or successor will want to know that they're taking over a business with no hidden legal risks.

5. Maximize Profitability:

Before exiting, focus on **maximizing profitability**. This might mean cutting unnecessary expenses, negotiating better deals with suppliers, or increasing your pricing strategy. The more profitable **TechZone** is, the more attractive it will be to buyers and the higher the valuation you'll receive.

Vinu: That's a great roadmap, Manu. It's clear that I need to make sure **TechZone** is running smoothly and is financially healthy before I consider exiting. It sounds like a lot of preparation goes into a successful exit.

Manu: Exactly, Vinu! Planning your **exit strategy** early gives you the time to build a valuable, well-structured business that attracts the right buyers or successors. Whether you plan to sell, pass it on, or step back, having a strong exit plan and understanding the value of **TechZone** ensures that you get the best outcome when the time comes.

Chapter 10 - Growth and Succession Planning

10.1 Financial Planning for Growth

10.2 Succession Planning and Business Continuity

10.1 Financial Planning for Growth

Vinu: Manu, I've been thinking a lot about how to make TechZone grow, but I feel like I need a clear financial plan to guide that growth. I want to make sure we're allocating resources effectively and planning for the long term. Can you walk me through how to create a financial strategy that will support the business as it expands?

Manu: Of course, Vinu! A solid financial plan is key to sustainable growth. It helps you allocate resources, prepare for risks, and take advantage of opportunities as they come. Let's break down how to create a financial plan for TechZone that supports your goals and keeps the business on track.

Step 1: Set Clear Growth Goals

Manu: First, you need to set specific growth goals for TechZone. Think about what you want to achieve. Are you looking to grow revenue, expand into new markets, or launch new products? Setting clear goals will give you direction.

Vinu: Okay, I'd like to grow revenue by 20% over the next year and maybe expand into two new regions. I'm also thinking about launching a new product line within the next 18 months.

Manu: Great! These goals will shape your financial plan. Let's take the revenue growth goal, for example. To grow revenue by 20%, you'll need to think about how many more customers you'll need, what sales channels to use, and how much to invest in marketing to reach them. For expanding into new regions, you'll need to consider costs like hiring new staff, setting up logistics, and advertising in those areas.

Step 2: Forecast Revenue and Expenses

Manu: Now that you have your goals, the next step is to forecast your revenue and expenses. This will give you a picture of what's needed to reach those goals.

Vinu: So, I need to estimate how much money we'll make and how much we'll need to spend?

Manu: Exactly. Let's start with revenue. If you're aiming for a 20% revenue increase, break that down by quarter. Say you expect to grow by 5% each quarter. Figure out how many more units you need to sell to hit that target. For instance, if TechZone makes ₹10,00,000 per quarter now, you'd be aiming for ₹10,50,000 next quarter.

Now, for expenses, think about the costs tied to this growth. Are you planning to hire new staff? Increase marketing? You'll also want to include costs for launching your new product line—research, development, and marketing.

Vinu: I get it. So if we're expanding into new regions, I need to factor in extra costs like salaries for new hires, marketing in those areas, and possibly new office space.

Step 3: Allocate Capital Strategically

Manu: Once you have a forecast, it's time to decide where to invest your resources. You want to put money into areas that will give you the highest return.

Vinu: How do I figure out which areas to prioritize?

Manu: Look at where you can get the most growth. For instance, if expanding into a new region could boost your sales by 30%, that's a high-return opportunity. Invest in marketing, sales teams, and local partnerships for those regions. At the same time, keep a balance between short-term and long-term investments.

Vinu: So I should focus on immediate growth like new regions, but also invest in things like product development that may take longer to pay off?

Manu: Exactly. Also, make sure to keep a cash reserve. Growth can come with unexpected expenses, so having a financial cushion will help you stay stable. For example, if TechZone's new product launch gets delayed, that reserve can cover costs until you start seeing revenue.

Step 4: Consider Funding Options

Vinu: What if my cash flow isn't enough to cover all these growth initiatives?

Manu: That's when you might look into financing options. If you need a large amount upfront for expansion, you could consider a loan or even bring in investors. For example, if TechZone needs ₹10,00,000 to expand into new regions, a loan could help cover those costs, and you'd repay it over time.

Vinu: I see. But I need to be careful about taking on too much debt, right?

Manu: Yes. Make sure any financing aligns with your long-term goals. Only borrow if the expected return from the growth is higher than the cost of the loan. Otherwise, consider equity investment, but remember, that would mean sharing ownership.

Step 5: Monitor and Adjust the Plan

Manu: The last step is to regularly review your financial plan. Growth doesn't always go as expected, so you'll need to adapt.

Vinu: How often should I review it?

Manu: At least quarterly. Check your key metrics like revenue, profit margins, and customer acquisition costs. If something is off, adjust your plan. For example, if your revenue in a new region isn't meeting targets, you might need to invest more in local marketing or adjust your pricing.

Vinu: So, it's not a "set it and forget it" plan. I need to make changes as things develop.

Manu: Exactly. Growth is a journey, and the plan is your guide. Stay flexible and keep an eye on the market. If TechZone's sales start exceeding projections, you might want to allocate even more resources to scale up quickly.

Vinu: That makes sense. I'll track our progress and adjust the plan as needed. It's reassuring to know that I can stay on course even if things change.

Putting It All Together

Manu: To recap, here's how to create a financial plan for growth:

- **Set specific goals** – Whether it's revenue growth, market expansion, or launching new products, clear goals will guide your plan.

- **Forecast revenue and expenses** – Estimate your earnings and costs based on those goals so you know what to expect financially.

- **Allocate capital wisely** – Invest in high-return areas, balance short- and long-term investments, and maintain a cash reserve.

- **Consider funding options** – If you need more capital, explore loans or equity, but make sure it aligns with your growth strategy.

- **Monitor and adjust** – Regularly check your key metrics and adjust the plan to stay on track.

Vinu: Thanks, Manu! This gives me a clear roadmap for planning TechZone's growth. I'll make sure to set goals, forecast accurately, and keep an eye on the numbers as we expand.

Manu: You've got it, Vinu! With a solid financial plan in place, you're setting TechZone up for sustainable growth. Remember, the key is to stay adaptable and make informed decisions as you go.

10.2 Succession Planning and Business Continuity

Vinu: Manu, I've been thinking about what would happen to TechZone if I ever had to step back or if something unexpected happened. I want to make sure the business can keep running smoothly, even if I'm not there. How do I plan for succession and ensure business continuity?

Manu: That's a smart move, Vinu! Succession planning and business continuity are essential. They help make sure that TechZone can keep going strong, whether you decide to step down, sell the business, or face an unexpected event. Let's walk through how you can plan for a smooth leadership transition and prepare the business to handle any situation.

What is Succession Planning?

Manu: Succession planning is about figuring out who will take over the business when you're not there. It could be a family member, a key employee, or even an outside leader. The goal is to ensure that TechZone has someone ready to step in and lead effectively.

Here's why it's important:

- **Smooth Leadership Transition**: With a plan in place, the new leader can step in with confidence, whether you're handing over the reins gradually or need a quick transition.

- **Reduces Disruption**: Changes in leadership can cause uncertainty. A succession plan helps TechZone keep running smoothly, minimizing confusion for employees, customers, and stakeholders.

- **Increases Business Value**: If you ever want to sell TechZone, having a clear succession plan makes the business more appealing to buyers and investors, as it shows that the company can thrive without you.

- **Prepares for the Unexpected**: Life is unpredictable. A succession plan ensures TechZone is ready to handle unforeseen events, like illness or emergencies, without missing a beat.

Vinu: So, it's about making sure the business runs smoothly, whether I step back by choice or if something unexpected happens. How do I start planning?

Step 1: Identify Potential Successors

Manu: First, you need to identify who might take over. Start by looking at the people around you—your management team, key employees, or family members. Here's how:

- **Internal Candidates**: Look at your team. Is there someone who understands TechZone's vision and operations? For example, if you have a capable COO or head of sales who's been with you for a while, they could be strong candidates.

- **Family Members**: If TechZone is a family business, you might want to groom a family member to take over. Make sure they're interested and have the right skills. If not, you can always develop those skills through mentoring and training.

- **External Candidates**: Sometimes, bringing in an outsider makes sense, especially if they bring new ideas and experience. Just make sure they align with TechZone's culture and values.

- **Leadership Pipeline**: Even if you're not stepping down soon, start building a pipeline by identifying and nurturing employees with leadership potential. For TechZone, you could set up mentoring programs or offer leadership training to help them grow.

Vinu: I get it. I need to look both inside and outside the company and start developing people now. What's the next step after identifying potential successors?

Step 2: Train and Prepare Successors

Manu: Now it's time to prepare them for the role. Here's how:

- **Hands-On Experience**: Involve them in key projects and decisions. For example, let your potential successor lead a product launch or manage relationships with important clients. This way, they get a feel for what it's like to run TechZone.

- **Mentorship**: Spend time sharing your insights, experience, and vision for TechZone. Walk them through your thought process, and help them develop the skills they need to lead.

- **Cross-Department Training**: Make sure they understand all parts of the business. For instance, if your successor has been in sales, expose them to finance, operations, and product development. In TechZone, if they've been working in product development, give them a chance to learn about customer service and supply chain management.

- **Set Clear Expectations**: Let them know the timeline and what's expected of them. For example, you could tell them that over the next two years, they'll gradually take on more leadership responsibilities, with the goal of stepping into a full leadership role in three years.

Vinu: That makes sense. Preparing them now gives me confidence that they'll be ready when the time comes. But what if the transition has to happen suddenly?

Step 3: Plan for Business Continuity

Manu: Good point, Vinu. Business continuity is all about ensuring TechZone keeps running smoothly, even if something unexpected happens. Here's what to do:

- **Document Key Processes**: Make sure all important processes are well-documented. This includes things like financial procedures, sales processes, and supplier relationships. For example, write down how day-to-day operations are managed and who is responsible for each task. This way, if someone has to step in, they can follow the process without confusion.

- **Create an Emergency Team**: Set up a team of key managers who can run the business temporarily. For TechZone, you could have a group consisting of your CFO, COO, and head of sales ready to step in if needed. They can keep the business steady until a permanent leader takes over.

- **Develop a Crisis Plan**: Create a plan that outlines how TechZone will respond to unexpected events, whether it's a leadership change or a market disruption. Regularly review and update this plan to make sure it's relevant.

- **Build Financial Reserves**: Ensure TechZone has enough cash on hand to handle disruptions. For example, if a sudden change occurs, having cash reserves means you can cover expenses and keep operations running smoothly.

- **Communicate with Stakeholders**: Let your employees, customers, and key partners know about your continuity plan. For instance, you might reassure major clients that there's a solid plan in place for TechZone to keep operating no matter what happens.

Vinu: I like the idea of having an emergency team and making sure our key processes are documented. It's good to know that TechZone can continue smoothly, even if something unexpected happens. What's the last step?

Step 4: Execute the Transition When Ready

Manu: When the time comes to hand over the business, here's how to make the transition as smooth as possible:

- **Gradual Transition**: If you can, make it gradual. Start by handing over day-to-day tasks and let your successor take on more responsibilities over time. You could remain involved as an advisor while they take charge of the daily operations.

- **Communicate Clearly**: Let your team know well in advance. For TechZone, you might announce that over the next year, your successor will be stepping into a leadership role while you gradually step back. Clear communication reduces uncertainty and helps employees feel comfortable with the change.

- **Monitor the Transition**: Stay involved to offer guidance and support. Answer questions, provide feedback, and make sure your successor feels confident in their new role.

- **Celebrate the Transition**: Acknowledge this significant milestone for both you and TechZone. A public announcement can also help build confidence among employees, customers, and partners.

Vinu: I like the idea of a gradual transition—it'll give everyone time to adjust. And I'll definitely make sure to communicate the plan clearly so that our team feels secure.

Manu: Exactly, Vinu. Succession planning and business continuity ensure that TechZone can thrive, even if you're not directly involved. By preparing early and setting up a strong continuity plan, you're positioning the business for long-term success.

Conclusion: Integrated Financial Strategy

Vinu: Manu, after everything we've discussed, I'm starting to see how important it is to have a fully integrated financial strategy for TechZone. I understand different pieces like growth planning, managing cash flow, and succession, but I'm still not clear on how to bring it all together. Also, I want to make sure we're prepared for any unexpected risks that might come our way.

Manu: That's a great observation, Vinu! An integrated financial strategy means tying all those parts together so they support TechZone's long-term success. It's about aligning your financial decisions with your goals and managing risks to keep the business stable, no matter what happens. Let's break it down step-by-step.

Step 1: Align Financial Goals with Business Strategy

Manu: To get started, make sure your financial goals support TechZone's overall growth plans. Every rupee you spend should be driving your business forward. If you're looking to expand into new regions, for example, you'll need to prioritize funds for marketing, hiring, and setting up operations in those areas.

Vinu: So it's about making sure that everything we're spending is in line with where we want to go?

Manu: Exactly. This alignment makes your financial plan more effective and ensures that every decision is moving you closer to your goals. If your main goal is expanding into new markets, focus your spending on things that help achieve that, like reaching new customers or building local partnerships.

Step 2: Holistic Financial Management

Manu: Think of your financial strategy as the big picture where cash flow, profitability, tax planning, and investments all work together. For example, if TechZone's goal is to increase revenue, your strategy should involve:

- **Managing Cash Flow**: Make sure there's enough cash on hand to support growth and handle any short-term needs. Keep an eye on receivables and make sure you're collecting payments promptly.

- **Tax Planning**: Ensure you're taking advantage of any tax benefits or deductions. For example, if TechZone invests in new equipment, you might be able to claim depreciation to reduce your taxable income.

- **Reinvesting Profits**: Instead of taking out profits for personal use, consider reinvesting them back into the business. For TechZone, this could mean using profits to launch new products or improve existing ones.

Vinu: So, all these elements - cash flow, taxes, and reinvestments - should work together to support our bigger goals?

Manu: Exactly. By looking at these elements as parts of a whole, you'll have a financial strategy that's aligned with TechZone's growth objectives.

Step 3: Risk Management and Contingency Planning

Vinu: How do we plan for risks in a way that fits into this bigger strategy?

Manu: Risk Management is about identifying what could go wrong and making sure TechZone is prepared. Here's how you can build it into your financial strategy:

- **Identify Financial Risks**: Start by figuring out what could impact TechZone. This could include:

- **Market Risks**: Things like economic downturns or new competitors that affect sales.

- **Operational Risks**: Issues in the supply chain, equipment malfunctions, or staffing shortages.

- **Financial Risks**: Changes in interest rates, currency fluctuations, or cash flow challenges.

For example, if TechZone relies on a few key suppliers, what would happen if one of them faced issues? Identifying these risks lets you plan ahead.

- **Develop Contingency Plans**: Once you've identified risks, create backup plans. For example:

  o Have a second supplier lined up in case there's a disruption with the primary one.

  o Create a cost-cutting plan for when sales slow down, so you can maintain profitability.

  o Set up a line of credit to ensure TechZone has access to funds during tough times.

These plans mean that when something unexpected happens, TechZone can adapt without missing a beat.

- **Build Financial Resilience**: Make sure TechZone has a financial cushion. This could mean keeping a cash reserve or diversifying your revenue streams. For example, if TechZone has reliable income from multiple products, you'll be less vulnerable if demand drops for one of them.

- **Regularly Review and Update**: Risk management isn't something you do once and forget. You'll need to regularly review and update your contingency plans to reflect changes in TechZone's operations or the market. If you're expanding into new areas, new risks will come up, so keep your plans flexible.

- **Communicate with Your Team**: Make sure your team knows about your risk management plans. This keeps everyone prepared and avoids confusion if something goes wrong. For TechZone, you might hold regular team meetings to discuss these plans, so everyone knows what to do in a crisis.

Vinu: So, by preparing for risks and having backup plans, TechZone can keep moving forward even when challenges come up.

Manu: Exactly. With risk management and contingency plans, you're building a resilient business that can handle unexpected situations.

Step 4: Keep Your Strategy Flexible

Manu: The final piece is flexibility. TechZone needs to be ready to adapt as things change. Regularly monitor your financial performance, track your key metrics, and make adjustments when necessary.

For example:

- If sales dip, consider slowing down on expansion and focus on boosting cash flow.

- If expenses rise unexpectedly, review your budget and find areas to cut costs without impacting your goals.

- If TechZone has a good month with higher-than-expected profits, think about reinvesting some of that back into growth opportunities, like new product development or marketing.

Vinu: So it's about continuously monitoring and being ready to adjust the plan as needed?

Manu: Exactly. Growth isn't a straight path, so you have to stay flexible. An integrated financial strategy means keeping an eye on everything, from cash flow and investments to risks and opportunities. This way, you're always prepared to make smart decisions.

Putting It All Together

Manu: Here's how it all connects, Vinu:

- **Align Financial Goals**: Every decision you make should support TechZone's growth goals, like expanding into new markets or launching new products.

- **Manage Cash Flow and Finances Holistically**: Look at your cash flow, tax planning, and reinvestment strategy as a whole to ensure you're supporting long-term growth.

- **Plan for Risks**: Identify potential risks and have backup plans so TechZone can keep running smoothly, no matter what.

- **Stay Flexible**: Monitor your performance regularly and adjust your plans as needed. Growth comes with ups and downs, so adaptability is key.

Vinu: This really helps me see the bigger picture. By making sure all parts of the strategy are connected and having plans for risks, I'm setting TechZone up for long-term success.

Manu: Absolutely, Vinu! An integrated financial strategy keeps TechZone on a steady path to growth. You're building a business that's not only focused on growth but also resilient to challenges. This approach sets TechZone up to thrive in the future, no matter what comes your way.

Achieving Financial Mastery

Vinu: Manu, I feel like I've learned so much from our conversations. But now that we've covered everything, how do I bring it all together and apply it to my business?

Manu: I'm glad to hear that, Vinu! It's been quite a journey, hasn't it? The key now is to take everything you've learned and apply it step by step. Financial mastery doesn't happen overnight, but with consistent effort, you'll start seeing the results in your business.

Vinu: I agree. But sometimes I feel overwhelmed by all the concepts—cash flow, profitability, risk management, exit strategies. Where do I start?

Manu: That's understandable, Vinu. It's a lot to take in, but the most important thing is to start with the basics and build from there. Begin by focusing on the day-to-day management of your finances. Here's a simple roadmap to get started:

- **Cash Flow and Liquidity**: Ensure you have a firm grip on your cash flow. Regularly review your cash flow statements and forecasts to avoid surprises. Make sure your business has enough liquidity to cover short-term obligations.

- **Profitability:** Keep an eye on your profit margins. Look for ways to improve your gross and net margins by managing costs and optimizing pricing strategies. A profitable business is a sustainable business.

- **Working Capital**: Regularly monitor your working capital. Maintain a balance between receivables, inventory, and payables. Efficient working capital management ensures that your business has the funds it needs for day-to-day operations.

- **Debt and Leverage:** Use debt wisely. Don't take on more than your business can handle, and always calculate your Debt Service Coverage Ratio (DSCR) to ensure you're not over-leveraging.

- **Financial Ratios**: Use financial ratios to track your business's health. These ratios give you insights into profitability, liquidity, and efficiency. Reviewing them quarterly will help you spot trends and make informed decisions.

Vinu: That sounds like a good plan. So, by focusing on these areas, I can improve my business's financial health over time?

Manu: Exactly. Financial management is all about staying proactive. As you apply these concepts, you'll gain confidence in handling your business's finances. Over time, you'll be better prepared to make larger decisions, whether it's about growth, raising capital, or even planning for your business's future exit.

Vinu: Speaking of the future, what's the most important thing I should keep in mind as I plan for the long term?

Manu: The most important thing is to always have a clear financial strategy. Whether it's budgeting for the year, planning for expansion, or thinking about your exit strategy, your financial decisions should align with your business goals. Never let your finances drift—always keep them aligned with your vision for growth and sustainability.

Also, stay flexible. The business landscape changes, and you need to be able to adapt. Regularly reviewing your financial plan will help you stay on course, even when challenges arise.

Vinu: I've learned a lot about financial clarity from this journey. It feels like I have a clear roadmap now, and I know what to focus on moving forward.

Manu: That's great to hear, Vinu. Remember, financial mastery is a continuous process. As your business grows, you'll face new challenges and opportunities, but with the right financial mindset, you'll be able to handle them with confidence.

Vinu: Thank you, Manu. I'm ready to take everything I've learned and apply it to my business. I feel much more prepared to make financial decisions now.

Manu: You're welcome, Vinu! It's been a pleasure guiding you through this journey. Remember, the tools are all in your hands now. Keep learning, stay proactive, and you'll achieve financial mastery in no time.

Vinu: I'll do my best. Here's to a financially sound future for my business!

Final Thoughts from the Author

As you've seen through Manu and Vinu's journey, financial clarity is not just about understanding numbers—it's about using that knowledge to make better decisions for your business. Every entrepreneur faces financial challenges, but with the right tools and strategies, you can navigate those challenges with confidence.

Take what you've learned in this book and start applying it to your business today. Whether it's managing cash flow, optimizing profitability, or planning for the future, these principles will help you build a financially strong, resilient business.

If you wish to learn more in detail, explore our pre-recorded online course "Financial Literacy for Entrepreneurs" – exclusively designed for Entrepreneurs. Scan to know more:

Wishing you success in your entrepreneurial journey!

- CA N Raja

Key financial reports entrepreneurs should review to stay on top of their business's financial health at various intervals:

1) Daily

Cash Flow Report: Monitor cash inflows and outflows to ensure liquidity.

Sales Report: Track daily sales to understand revenue trends.

Accounts Receivable Aging Report: Check overdue customer payments to keep cash flow healthy.

Inventory Levels Report: Ensure stock levels are adequate to meet demand without overstocking.

2) Weekly

Accounts Payable Aging Report: Track pending supplier payments and upcoming due dates.

Weekly Profit and Loss (P&L) Statement: Analyze revenue, cost of goods sold, and expenses to gauge profitability.

Payroll Report (if applicable): Confirm payroll calculations and total labor costs for the week.

Sales Pipeline Report: Review potential deals and sales leads in the pipeline to project near-term revenue.

Customer Complaints or Feedback Report: Identify any recurring issues with products or services.

3) Monthly

Monthly Profit and Loss (P&L) Statement: Evaluate profitability and trends in revenue, expenses, and cost of goods sold.

Balance Sheet: Assess assets, liabilities, and equity to understand the financial position of the business.

Cash Flow Statement: Review cash inflows and outflows from operating, investing, and financing activities.

Budget vs. Actual Report: Compare actual results to the budget to spot discrepancies and control spending.

Inventory Turnover Report: Analyze how quickly inventory is moving, indicating sales performance and stock management efficiency.

Key Performance Indicators (KPIs): Track metrics like gross profit margin, net profit margin, and current ratio for monthly progress.

Accounts Receivable and Payable Aging Reports: Monitor receivables and payables to maintain cash flow.

Sales and Marketing Expense Report: Evaluate the cost-effectiveness of marketing efforts and adjust as needed.

4) Quarterly

Quarterly P&L Statement: Review quarterly trends in revenue, expenses, and net income.

Cash Flow Statement (Quarterly): Understand the cash position over the quarter to manage liquidity.

Balance Sheet (Quarterly): Assess changes in assets, liabilities, and equity.

Statement of Changes in Equity: Track owners' equity over the quarter due to profits or losses and any investments or withdrawals.

Customer Profitability Report: Identify high-value customers and adjust focus based on customer profitability analysis.

Employee Performance Report: Review productivity and labor efficiency, especially if payroll is a significant expense.

Sales Analysis by Region/Product/Service: Analyze which areas or products are performing well and allocate resources accordingly.

Debt and Interest Payment Report: Monitor debt levels and interest payments to manage financial leverage.

5) Half-Yearly

Half-Yearly P&L Statement: Evaluate year-to-date profitability and adjust strategies as needed.

Comparative Balance Sheet: Compare the financial position with the previous half-year to observe growth or issues.

Cash Flow Projection Report: Project cash flows for the next six months based on past data.

Break-Even Analysis: Calculate the break-even point to assess profitability in relation to costs and pricing.

Market Position and Competitive Analysis: Review industry and market trends to remain competitive.

Tax Preparation Report: Ensure compliance with tax liabilities and prepare for potential payments or refunds.

Capital Expenditure Analysis: Evaluate return on significant investments in assets or infrastructure.

6) Annual

Annual P&L Statement: Assess the overall profitability for the year and identify growth opportunities or areas to cut costs.

Balance Sheet (Year-End): Review the company's financial position at year-end to understand assets, liabilities, and equity.

Cash Flow Statement (Annual): Get a complete view of cash inflows and outflows throughout the year.

Annual Budget and Forecast Report: Set financial targets for the coming year based on past performance.

Income Tax Return: Review the tax liability, ensuring all tax records are accurate and compliant.

Financial Ratios Analysis: Review key ratios such as debt-to-equity, current ratio, ROE, and ROA to analyze financial health.

Auditor's Report (if applicable): Get an external auditor's perspective on the financial statements and internal controls.

Employee Compensation and Benefits Review: Ensure that compensation is competitive and aligned with business goals.

Strategic Plan Review: Align financial strategies with business goals, and set objectives for the next year.

Customer and Market Analysis: Analyze customer demographics, spending patterns, and market position for long-term planning.

www.ingramcontent.com/pod-product-compliance
Lightning Source LLC
Chambersburg PA
CBHW040732120726
48010CB00002B/94